Nursery Décor

Projects for Decorating Your Baby's Room

Debra Quartermain

Published by

Krause Publications
700 E. State St.,
Iola, WI 54990-0001

Please call or write for our free catalog of publications. Our toll-free number to place
an order or obtain a free catalog is 800-258-0929, or please use our regular business
telephone 715-445-2214.

Project designs by Debra Quartermain.
Photography by Glen D. Ross, unless otherwise noted.
Photography on pages 3 and 126, and author photo on back cover by Joslyn Daigle.
Illustrations by Charles C. Bliss.

Library of Congress Catalog Number: 2002105103

ISBN: 0-87349-496-2

Unique Projects You Can Make for the Children in Your Life

Sew & Go Baby
A Collection of Practical Baby Gear Projects
by Jasmine Hubble

Presents 30 practical projects for you to assemble a memorable gift or party for the special baby or toddler in your life. Clear directions, easy-to-follow patterns and full-color photography will enable you to create an entire baby shower, essential baby gear, clothes, accessories and thoughtful sibling gifts.

Softcover • 8-1/4 x 10-7/8 • 96 pages
300 illustrations
Item# SFTB • $19.95

Fast Patch® Kids' Quilts
Dozens of Designs To Make for and with Kids
by Anita Hallock and Betsy Hallock Heath

The unique Fast Patch® technique allows you to create checkerboards and tricky triangles from simple sewn strips. Kids will love the 20 different quilt blocks featuring birds, fish, butterflies and clowns. Margin symbols tell you when kids can help, too!

Softcover • 8-1/4 x 10-7/8 • 112 pages
color section
Item# FPKQ • $22.95

Sew & Go Kids
by Jasmine Hubble

If you love to sew comfortable, fashionable clothing for your kids, but don't have a lot of time, this is the perfect book for you! The author of *Sew & Go* and *Sew & Go Baby* gives you more than 30 fun, practical projects like vests, pants, skirts, and pajamas (sizes 2 to 8), and, as a bonus, great ideas for play-time, like a puppet theater and stuffed animal tent. Includes simple step-by-step instructions, helpful illustrations, and full-size patterns.

Softcover • 8-1/4 x 10-7/8 • 96 pages
100 color photos
Item# SWKI • $21.95

Kids 1st Summer Crafts
by Krause Publications

How many times have you heard "I'm bored" from your children during the summer? No more! In this brand-new booklet kids ages 5 to 13 will find hours of enjoyment from 20 different crafts, games and activities, designed especially for them. With easy-to-follow instructions and projects suitable for all skill levels, this idea book will keep your kids going all summer long!

Softcover • 8-1/4 x 10-7/8 • 24 pages
25 color photos
Item# K1SC • $6.95

Ultimate Scrapbook Guide
by Julie Stephani

The fourth book in the best-selling More than Memories series is here! Master-scrapbooker Julie Stephani answers the most often asked questions about scrapbooking. Included are hundreds of creative scrapbooking ideas and projects, expert tips and advice on a wide variety of techniques.

Softcover • 8-1/4 x 10-7/8
128 pages
color throughout
Item# MTM4 • $19.95

Shape Your Memories
Creating One-of-a-Kind Scrapbook Pages
by Patti Swoboda

Add new dimension to your scrapbook pages with Patti Swoboda's innovative, new technique! Through step-by-step instructions and photographs, you'll quickly learn how to use common scrapbooking tools and Staedtler's Hot Foil Pen to create shaped pages and page protectors. Features 13 projects and variations.

Softcover • 8-1/4 x 10-7/8 • 48 pages
75 color photos & more than 50 full-size patterns
Item# SYM • $10.95

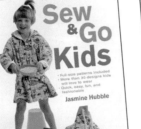

To order call **800-258-0929** Offer CRB2
M-F 7am - 8pm • Sat 8am - 2pm, CST

Shipping & Handling: $4.00 first book, $2.25 each additional. Non-US addresses $20.95 first book, $5.95 each additional.
Sales Tax: CA, IA, IL, NJ, PA, TN, VA, WI residents please add appropriate sales tax.
Satisfaction Guarantee: If for any reason you are not completely satisfied with your purchase, simply return it within 14 days of receipt and receive a full refund, less shipping charges.

Krause Publications
Offer CRB2
P.O. Box 5009
Iola WI 54945-5009

www.krausebooks.com

Express Your Personal Style

128

Embroidery Machine Essentials
How to Stabilize, Hoop and Stitch Decorative Designs
by Jeanine Twigg, Foreword by Lindee Goodall

Frustrated by the lack of information in your embroidery machine's instruction manual? This book will help you learn how to use your embroidery machine to its fullest potential. From choosing threads to knowing which stabilizer to pair with your fabric, you'll find helpful tips and techniques for producing creative designs. Learn to successfully hoop and stitch designs and put these skills to use creating 20 simple projects. Includes a free CD featuring 6 exclusive embroidery designs digitized by award-winning Lindee Goodall, owner of Cactus Punch®.

Softcover • 8-1/4 x 10-7/8 • 144 pages
250+ color photos and illustrations
Item# STIT • $27.95

Embracing Child Art
Projects for Grown-ups to Keep and Treasure
by Barbara A. McGuire

Celebrate children's artistic expressions with the unique ideas presented by Barbara A. McGuire in this exciting new book. You'll learn how to transform your child's drawings into functional pieces you can cherish forever—from an Op Art Lantern to elegant jewelry. Learn the basic principles of design and explore a variety of media applications such as polymer clay, paper, ceramics, glass, wood, paint and more.

Softcover • 8-1/4 x 10-7/8 • 144 pages
200 color photos and illustrations
Item# CHART • $24.95

Nancy Cornwell's Polar Magic
New Adventures With Fleece
by Nancy Cornwell

Join award-winning author Nancy Cornwell on another exciting and educational sewing adventure with fleece—one of today's hottest fabrics. Includes step-by-step instructions for 16 projects such as quilts, pillows, a jacket, vests and much more, plus 15 different templates for stitch patterns used to embellish garments. You will love the versatility and new twist put on fleece.

Softcover • 8-1/4 x 10-7/8 • 160 pages
200 color photos
Item# AWPF3 • $21.95

Granny Quilts
Vintage Quilts of the '30s Made New for Today
by Darlene Zimmerman

Make a gorgeous quilt, reminiscent of the 1930s, with the help of this creative new book. You'll explore the history and style of the '30s quilts, while learning to replicate them with reproduction fabrics and more than 12 beautiful projects. A variety of appliquéd and pieced quilts are featured with updated rotary cutting directions written for quilters of all skill levels.

Softcover • 8-1/4 x 10-7/8 • 128 pages
150+ color photos and illustrations
Item# GRANQ • $21.95

Creative Containers
The Resourceful Crafter's Guide
by Jill Evans

How many times have you heard "One man's trash is another man's treasure?" Well, in this new book, author Jill Evans shows you how to turn your recyclables into beautiful home décor items, useful containers and earth-friendly gifts. From things like tuna cans, vegetable cans and cookie tins, you'll create 50 unique projects such as a scarecrow, red-nosed reindeer, penguin, candleholder and leprechaun!

Softcover • 8-1/4 x 10-7/8 • 96 pages
75 color photos
Item# CRCONT • $14.95

Sewing With Nancy's Favorite Hints
20th Anniversary Edition
by Nancy Zieman

To celebrate the 20th anniversary of her popular PBS show, Nancy Zieman brings you a collection of her favorite tips, hints, and techniques from the past two decades. You'll find tips for keeping your sewing room organized, Nancy's favorite notions, helpful sewing solutions, embroidery hints, quilting tips, and more! Relive the memories of the longest-running sewing program on public television with the nation's leading sewing authority!

Softcover • 8-1/4 x 10-7/8 • 144 pages
150 color photos
Item# NFTT • $19.95

Dedication and Acknowledgments

I remember being a little girl designing paper houses and sewing doll clothes. My parents, Bessie and Allan Quartermain, encouraged my creativity. For that I'll be forever grateful.

There are special people in my life who have believed in my talents and cheered me on—my brother Bob, my best friends Donna, Linda, Sharon, and Lorine; and Alison, who pushed me to take a big leap of faith and really test my abilities.

This book would have not been possible without several talented people. My photographer, Glen Ross, brought my designs to life perfectly. Charles Bliss transformed my rough illustrations, and Joslyn Daigle captured my daughters and me so happily on film. Thank you Appleby's and Harvey's for your quality service.

Many friends in the industry have provided me with helpful advice, products, and supplies. Thank you Julie, Sharon, Diane, Linda, Marie, Barb, Amy, Miriam, Samantha, and Jacqueline.

To Krause Publications, thank you for this amazing opportunity. To Julie Stephani for making a wish come true, and to Jodi Rintelman, my editor, and Marilyn Hochstatter, graphic designer, for their creative expertise to make a dream become reality.

I consider myself blessed to have many loving and caring people in my life. I know I am truly blessed by my two greatest gifts in this world—my beautiful, talented, and creative daughters, Amanda and Katy. They inspired the essence of this book—love.

Contents

All of life is a creative process. From homes to gardens, we design elements for ourselves every day. Many of us take specific materials and combine them to create decorative and useful items. In all of life, the most amazing creation is a baby, a special tiny bundle that arrives to fill our lives with joys and dreams.

In anticipation of a baby's arrival, we want to create a warm, magical place filled with color and cuddly animals, the perfect nursery. Both of my wonderful daughters, Amanda and Katy, are adopted and arrived at only a few days old. Waiting for them, six years and then almost another ten, gave me lots of time to decorate their nurseries. In fact, I must admit, I redecorated a couple of times before each one arrived.

Sometimes I would sit in their rooms just looking around, deciding what to add and enjoying the sweet charm of it all. I realized in doing this that nurseries are as much for parents as for the babies. We spend precious time in this room with our little ones. It's a place to let our imagination wander, where bunnies can hop across walls and teddy bears play ball. A rainbow of delicious colors can flow across walls and furniture in fanciful design.

I never would have dreamed that 20 years later I would be writing a book inspired by my most beloved joys, my two beautiful daughters. Creating wall hangings, pillows, toys, and curtains; painting whimsical murals and clouds for their rooms were hours spent in pure delight. As I designed the projects found in each of the rooms for this book, I have returned to those precious days many times.

To share soft cozy fabrics in dreamy colors and cuddly baby animals is a fantasy come true. So come inside and join the fun.

Chapter 1

Creating the Fantasy

Creating the Fantasy

In the pages of this book are many projects for four unique nurseries. As different as the rooms are the projects, which range from quick crafting to hand-embroidered blankets. This book isn't only for new parents, but also for grandmothers, other relatives, friends, or anyone who wants to create a special gift for baby. Give this book as a lovely shower gift, or use it as inspiration for a crafting baby shower.

Notes

Imagine

Create

In each chapter, there is a page for notes and comments, as this book becomes part of the memory keeping for baby. Perhaps this book will be passed on to the next generation, for these projects are as timeless in their appeal as babyhood.

Time these days seems to be a luxury for everyone, so many of the projects don't require a lot of time. The wide variety of projects was designed to fit every skill level and time frame. Techniques for working with different felts, foam, fabric, and adhesives are explained in this chapter. With some basic supplies, a few yards of fabric and felt, and some paint, anyone can create an imaginative, delightful, and truly special nursery.

Pull up a cozy rocker, relax, turn the pages, and imagine.

More Thoughts

Throughout the book I have included other suggestions for projects. My mind always seems to have "more thoughts" even once something is finished. These ideas are meant to give other options for a project. Hopefully some will inspire you to use the ideas to keep creating for the special baby in your life.

Materials and Tools

For any project, certain basic tools are necessary. Good quality tools will make projects easier. The projects in this book require a few tools, which I think are useful for any household in general. Once a baby arrives, there follow toy repairs, clothing adjustments, birthday decorations, Halloween costumes, school projects, and the list goes on. Invest in some good tools, and they will take you through the creative years ahead.

All the projects list supplies that are needed for each. Many use a lot of the same materials and tools, which I have described below. The products used are well-known brand items that should be available at your local craft or fabric shop. If you can't find a certain item, please refer to the source list at the back of the book. The company will then be able to direct you to a location for the product. Most companies have Web sites with this information and more about the product.

Felt: Kunin Felt's Rainbow Classic Felt™, Rainbow Plush Felt™, and Shaggy Plush Felt™. Kunin Felt products are available in a large array of colors from pastels to brights. All of the products are washable and can be line dried. Plush and shaggy felts become softer with washing. They don't ravel or fray.

Foam: STYROFOAM* brand foam pieces are sturdy lightweight shapes available in a large variety of round and flat designs. They cut easily with a knife, and they can be easily glued with a number of adhesives. Mold the edges by pressing your fingers along the edge area, or roll the area on the end of a counter or table. Sand the edges with another piece of foam.

Scissors: Fiskars® MicroTip, Softgrip®, Wave, Scallop, and Bent scissors. Their Softgrip scissors are easy on the hands. Fiskars also offers self-healing cutting mats, rotary cutters, and rulers, which are necessary for anyone working with fabrics on a regular basis.

Glues and adhesives: Adhesive Tech® glue gun and low temp. glue sticks, Beacon Fabri-Tac, Therm O Web PeelnStick Doublesided Adhesive and HeatnBond® UltraHold and Lite Iron-On Adhesive. All of these adhesives are excellent and instrumental in the success of almost every project in the book.

Sewing and embroidery threads: J. & P. Coats, Coats & Clark. Their upholstery thread is my favorite for a super strong thread to string joint animals and gather felt shapes.

Polyester fiberfill, batting, and pillow forms: Warm Company.

Acrylic paints and finishes: DecoArt™ Americana™ and Crafter's Acrylic™; DuraClear™ varnish.

Eye beads: John Bead Corp. Ltd.

Needles: The Colonial Needle Company.

Sewing machines: There are many brands of good sewing machines. For the projects in this book, a basic dependable machine is required.

*Trademark of The Dow Chemical Company.

Sewing with Plush Felt

With most projects that use plush and shaggy felts, I prefer to sew a smaller seam, usually ¼". The felt is thicker, and since it doesn't ravel, a narrow seam works well. If pressing is required, I use a cloth with classic felt. With plush and shaggy felts, I press very gently on the wrong side. The plush and shaggy felts have a nap, so run your hand over the felt to determine the direction. For most projects, the nap should run down. All the felts cut, sew, and glue easily. The felt has a slight give to it, which makes it a good choice for curved surfaces.

Covering Foam Shapes

Although I have worked with many craft products, my first love is design-ing and sewing three-dimensional soft figures, particularly animals—design, sew, and stuff. When I was first asked by Dow Chemical Company to create an animal that looked sewn but used foam shapes as a base, I didn't know if I could create that same soft cuddly effect with foam. I came up with a tech-nique that is easy and enables a complete non-sewer to craft a fuzzy animal that looks just like it was sewn. For someone who sews, it's a fun departure to work from the inside out. Just pick a foam shape and think, "What animal can I make today?"

Kunin Felt products work beautifully with many shapes of STYROFOAM brand foam. The felt has a slight stretch, which lends itself to the curves of balls and eggs. Both products cut and glue easily. Foam shapes can be cut with a serrated knife (my favorite is an old steak knife). I prefer using a glue gun and low temperature glue sticks with the foam. Other adhesives mentioned previously also work well. When using the glue gun, the foam may melt just slightly, which doesn't affect the success of the project at all.

When using the plush or shaggy felts, which have a nap, decide the direc-tion of the nap before cutting out the shape.

1 Cut a thin slice from one side of the ball or egg. Discard the thin slice. The shapes will be used in the following steps with this slice removed.

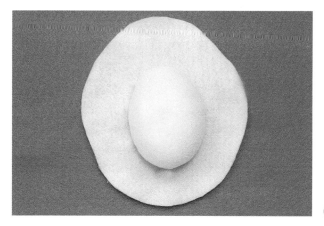

2 To cover the balls, refer to the chart for the appropriate circle size to cut from felt.

3 To cover an egg, lay it flat side down on the wrong side of the felt to use as a template. Measure and use a marker or pen to draw a line 2" from the edge of the egg. Draw with marker or pen. Cut out the felt, making sure to cut off the drawn lines. A disappearing marker is good to use on very light colored felt.

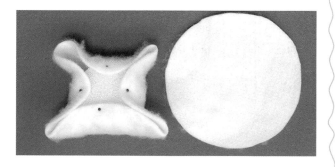

4 To cut a bottom for the ball or egg, place it on the felt, flat side down, and draw exactly around the shape. Cut out the felt, slightly to the inside of the drawn line.

5 Place the foam shape so the round side is centered on the wrong side of the cut felt piece. Bring the felt edges up and over the flat side. The felt should extend approximately an inch over the edge. If it overlaps at the center, trim off the excess. Pin the felt at the North, South, East, and West.

6 Remove a pin, and apply a thin line of glue in one small section. Push the felt into the glue, easing the excess by gathering slightly. There will be gathers on the sides, but this adds softness to the animal's body. Hold the glued felt to the foam for a few seconds until it dries. Repeat at the opposite side, pulling the felt smooth. (If you're not satisfied with the results, the felt will lift up again with a gentle pull.) If it's a large shape, some excess can be trimmed out in between the pins.

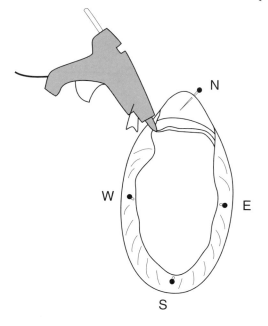

7 Glue the bottom to the flat side of the shape to finish.

Foam Ball Size	¾"	1"	1½"	2"	2½"	3"	4"	5"	6"
Felt Circle Size	2"	3"	4"	5"	6"	8"	10"	12"	16"

Creating the Fantasy

COVERING FLAT FOAM SHAPES

1 Use the shape as a template. Lay it down on the wrong side of the felt.

2 Measure and draw a line 2" from the edge of the shape. Cut out the felt, making sure to cut off the drawn lines. A disappearing marker is good to use on very light colored felt.

3 To cut a bottom for the shape, place it on the felt and draw exactly around the shape. Cut out slightly inside the drawn line.

4 Center the shape on the wrong side of the felt. Bring the felt up and over one side. With a thin line of glue close to the edge, press the felt into the foam. Hold for a few seconds.

5 Bring the felt up and over the opposite side. Glue it in place, pulling the felt smooth. Clip the curves, as shown in the photo.

6 Finish gluing the edges.

7 Glue the bottom piece to the shape.

Covering Flat Cardboard Shapes

1 Cut a pattern piece from lightweight cardboard and quilt batt. (For small pieces, glue the cardboard piece to the quilt batt, and then cut around it.)

2 Lay the cardboard piece on fabric or felt. Measure and draw a line 1" from the edge of the shape. Cut it out.

3 To cut a bottom for the shape, place it on the felt and draw exactly around the shape. Cut out slightly inside the drawn line.

4 Center the cardboard on the wrong side of the fabric with the quilt batt side down. Bring the fabric up over one side. With a thin line of glue close to the edge, press the fabric to the cardboard. Hold for a few seconds.

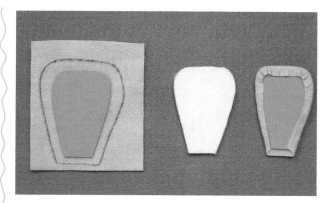

5 Bring the fabric up over the opposite side of the cardboard. Glue it in place, pulling the felt smooth. Clip the curves, as shown in photo.

6 Finish gluing the edges.

7 Glue the back piece to the shape.

Animal Features

INSERTING EYES

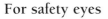

I believe the eyes are the most important aspect of any face you create. They bring a project to life. I prefer solid black eyes, which reflect light. Eyes also need to be inserted into a face so they round out only slightly on the front of the face.

There are several types of eyes. For animals that are going to be played with, safety eyes should be used. If the animal is to be used for decorative purposes only, an eye bead with a hole or a button-style eye with a shank can be used.

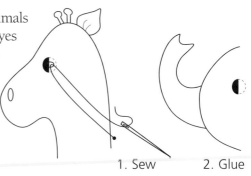

1. Sew   2. Glue

For safety eyes

Insert the eyes before the animal is stuffed. Make a small hole at each eye mark. Follow the manufacturer's directions.

For button eyes

1 Upholstery thread is a strong thread that can be used to anchor the eyes. A four to six inch soft sculpture needle will make it easy to stitch the eyes in place.

2 A small hole is made at each eye mark.

3 After the animal is stuffed, anchor the needle and thread securely at the bottom of the head or the back of the neck.

4 Take the needle out through the eye hole. Slip the needle through the shank, and take it back through the head, pulling the eye into the hole. Secure the thread. Repeat for the other eye.

For eye beads

1 Stuff the animal before inserting the eyes. Secure the needle and thread at the back of the neck.

2 Take the needle out through the face at the eye mark. Slide on the eye bead, and take the needle back through to the start.

3 Pull the stitches to indent the eye into the face. Repeat several times for the eye. Repeat the same for the second eye. Secure the thread at the start.

For glued eyes

1 With MicroTip scissors, make small holes through the felt into the foam at the eye marks.

2 Place a small dab of glue on the eye bead, and push it into the hole. One third of the eye bead should show. This gives a natural look to the face.

EAR PLEATING

Most animals have ears with a curved shape. Pleating the center of the ears creates this dimension.

1 Bring the lines together, and fold the center to one side.

2 Put glue along the bottom edge. Glue the ear in place.

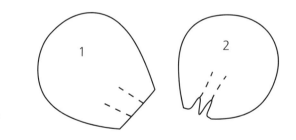

Embroidery Basics

Use embroidery needles. To keep floss from tangling when using more than one strand, separate the strands. Place the strands back together side by side. In several of the projects in the book, I have used my favorite three stitches—the outline or straight stitch, cross-stitch, and blanket stitch.

Straight stitch

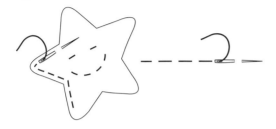

1 Close to the edge of the appliqué, bring the needle in and out continuously.

2 Keep the stitches small, straight, and even

Cross stitch

1 Create the first half of each stitch, left to right.

2 Complete other half by crossing stitches in opposite direction.

Blanket stitch

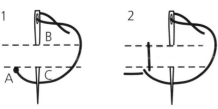

1 Come up at A, hold the thread with your thumb, go down at B and out at C.

2 Keep the tip of the needle over the thread and pull into place. Keep the vertical stitches as straight and even as you can.

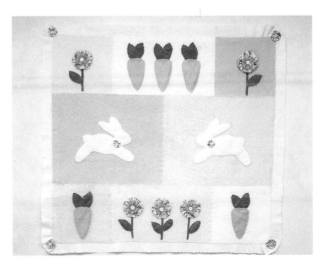

Creating a Yo-Yo

Yo-yos are a fun little sewing project that can be used to embellish just about everything. There is a relaxing quality to just sitting with a pile of colorful circles. Pick each one up, stitch over and over, and finish with a garden of soft flowers.

1 With strong thread, baste close to the outside edge of the circle.

2 Pull threads to secure.

3 Flatten the yo-yo with your fingers.

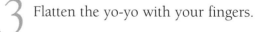

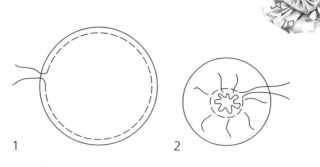

1   2

Simple Pillow Style

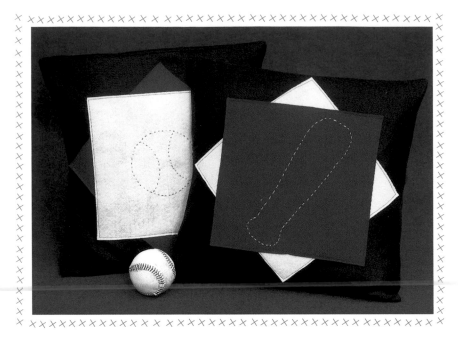

Working with felt to create pillows in this style is very simple. I like to make different covers for the seasons and simply change the cover, using the same pillow form each time.

1 Cut two pieces of felt. For the front, measure and draw a line 1" from the edge of the pillow form. Cut out the shape. For the back, measure and draw a line 2" from the edge of the pillow form. Cut out the shape. Cut this piece in half.

2 Overlap the two back pieces by 1". Lay the front piece on top. Pin.

3 Sew all around the sides, angling at the corners, as shown in the diagram.

4 Trim off all excess felt. Turn through the center opening.

5 Insert the pillow form.

6 Baste the opening shut, or fasten it with buttons, ties, or snaps.

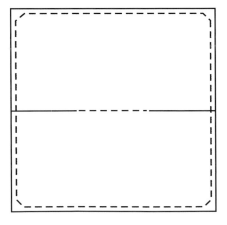

Nursery Décor

Stenciling

Today there are thousands of stencils and hundreds of accompanying products to accent any room, furniture piece, fabric, or almost any surface. There are many techniques, which include using sponges or brushes. The most important point to remember is to use very little paint, removing most of it on a paper towel before beginning to stencil.

This is my personal favorite style of stenciling, and it's the one used in the projects for this book. Many stencils come with directions and helpful hints.

1 Securely tape the stencil in place. If the fabric is to be stenciled, place a piece of cardboard underneath.

2 Hold the stencil brush straight up and down, and dip the end into acrylic paint. Dab off the paint on a paper towel until a soft smooth mark is made.

3 Hold the brush in the same up and down position. Begin stenciling along the edge in a circular motion.

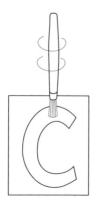

4 Work the paint into the center last, as the variation in color will give dimension to the design.

5 If you want more depth of color, go over the stencil again. Use another color to shade with, if desired.

6 Carefully lift the stencil off. If there is a little bleeding or smudging, move the stencil slightly and stencil the area. It won't be noticeable if fixed in this manner. If you're stenciling on wood or a wall, bleeding and smudges may wash off, if done immediately. Use a cotton swab along the edge.

7 Fabric can be heat set with an iron.

Nursery Décor

Chapter 2

The Enchanted Garden

What do little girls dream of?

Inside this enchanting room, the tiniest of little girls will dream sweet dreams surrounded by friendly bunnies, frilly flowers, and cozy comforts.

The gentle fresh colors of this room are like dear friends. I used them when decorating nurseries for both of my daughters. I spent many precious hours rocking them in their delightful rooms filled with whimsical accessories. Baby rooms are as much for parents as for babies, a magical retreat to enjoy special moments every day.

Wander into "The Enchanted Garden." Craft a flowerpot frame or sew a fuzzy cuddly bunny stuffed with love.

Bedtime Bunnies

Where do bunnies sleep? THEY SLEEP IN A CARROT BED, OF COURSE! THIS IS A FUN NO-SEW PROJECT THAT CAN BE THE INSPIRATION FOR MANY DELIGHTFUL STORIES. WHAT DO LITTLE BUNNIES DREAM OF...HMM.

SIZE: 13" LONG

YOU WILL NEED:

- Two 6" foam cones
- 9⅞" x 11⅞" x 1³⁄₁₆" foam block (cut in half)
- 2" foam ball
- 12" x 18" piece of cotton check
- 12" x 3" piece of a coordinating print
- 9" x 12" felt pieces: 4 Apricot, 2 Leaf Green, 1 White
- 9" x 11" Leaf Green plush felt
- 10" square white plush felt
- 4 oz. polyester fiberfill
- 4mm black eye bead

- 8 pastel ⅜" buttons
- 2 white ¾" pompoms
- 4 white ½" pompoms
- 3 pink ¼" pompoms
- 1 yd. black embroidery floss
- 3 white chenille stems

Tools: Scallop scissors, MicroTip scissors, glue gun and low temp. glue, embroidery needle, knife, blush, pins, pencil, marker, ruler.

1 Review the instructions for Covering Foam Shapes (page 10). Cut the required pattern pieces from the pattern sheet.

2 Cut the foam cones in half, and cut a slice off the foam balls.

3 To make the carrots, cover the cones with Apricot felt. To make the heads, cover the balls with White plush.

4 Cut two 3" x 5½" pieces of check fabric for the pillow. Set aside.

5 Cover the foam block with the remaining piece of check fabric, wrapping it like a present with the overlap glued underneath. Trim off any uneven ends.

6 Cut 24 carrot leaves from the Leaf Green felt. Cut each chenille stem into four pieces.

7 Start at the bottom of a leaf, and lay a chenille stem along the center of the leaf. Glue another leaf on top, sandwiching the chenille stem. Repeat for all leaves.

8 Use the point of the scissors to poke holes in the tops of the carrots. Squirt glue into the holes, and insert three leaves into each one.

9 Measure up 2½" on the flat sides of the carrots. With the flat sides in, glue the carrots to the ends of the block to create the bed frame. (If the bed is slightly wobbly, make a small slit in the fabric where it glues to the carrot, and squirt in extra glue.)

10 Cut the bunny ears out of White plush. Use scallop scissors to cut one 1½" x 11" strip, two 1½" x 7" strips, and ten 1" circles from the coordinating print fabric; cut ten ¾" circles from White felt.

11 With three strands of black embroidery floss, bring the needle from the back of the bunny's head through to the front. Make two ¼" stitches to create closed eyes. Tie the floss ends at the back of the head. For the last bunny

head, repeat for only one eye. Insert the other eye, as shown on page 14.

12 Pinch the opposite sides of the ear ends together. Place a small dot of glue at the end of each ear, and glue to the top of the head. Glue white pompoms together in pairs under the eyes. Glue pink noses on top of the white pompoms. Blush the ears and cheeks.

13 With right sides out, glue the pillow pieces together, leaving a small opening on one side. Gently stuff the pillow with fiberfill. Glue the opening shut. Trim around the edges with scallop scissors.

14 Glue the bunny heads side by side on the pillow.

15 Trim one 11" end of Leaf Green plush for the top of the blanket. Fold this edge over 1¾", and glue down. Glue a longer scallop-edged coordinating print fabric piece along this edge. Glue shorter pieces of fabric along the underside of the 9" edges.

16 Glue white felt circles on top of the fabric circles. Glue buttons in the center. Glue the circles to the top of the blanket in a random pattern.

17 Glue the pillow to the top of the bed. Place some fiberfill in the center of the bed. Center and glue the blanket over the bed, right under the bunny heads.

More Thoughts

MAKE EXTRA CARROT BEDPOSTS, AND STICK THEM OUT OF PRETTY PAINTED POTS OR A WINDOW BOX.

Garden Lap Quilt

In the evenings, cozy up with baby UNDER THIS COMFY QUILT. PART OF THE FUN OF BABIES IS THE EXCUSE THEY GIVE US TO RETURN TO CHILDHOOD MAGIC WHERE ANYTHING CAN HAPPEN. THIS WHIMSICAL QUILT IS COMPLETELY DONE BY HAND WITH THREE DIFFERENT STITCHES. IT'S AN EASY PROJECT TO PUT TOGETHER.

SIZE: 44" X 50"

Nursery Décor

YOU WILL NEED:

- ½ yd. plush felt in each color: Mint Green, Blush Pink, White
- ⅓ yd. Lemon Frost plush felt
- 9" x 12" felt pieces: 2 Leaf Green, 2 Apricot
- ½ yd. White felt
- 4" x 18" small floral print fabric
- ½ yd. coordinating large floral print fabric

- Skeins of embroidery floss: 2 pale green, 2 yellow, 3 white
- White upholstery thread
- 11 white ⅜" buttons

Tools: Wave-edge scissors, scissors, embroidery needle, sewing needle, pins, rotary cutter, cutting mat.

1 Review the tips for Sewing with Plush Felt (page 9); Embroidery Basics (page 16); and Creating a Yo-Yo (page 17). Cut the required pattern pieces from the pattern sheet. Cut 4" and 7" circle patterns for the yo-yos.

2 Cut the following pieces for the quilt:
Blush Pink—18" x 22", 12" x 12"
Mint Green—18" x 22", 12" x 12"
Lemon Frost—12" x 20", 12" x 12"
White plush—12" x 20", 12" x 12"

3 From the large floral print, cut five 7" circles and six 4" circles. From the small floral print, cut five 4" circles. Sew the yo-yos. Stack the small print ones on the large print ones. Sew buttons in the centers of all yo-yos.

4 Following the diagram, pin the shapes to each section. All single shapes are centered. The three shapes are evenly spaced in the 12" x 20" pieces.

5 Work on one piece at a time. Blanket stitch the carrots, bunny on pink, flower stems, and leaves with pale green floss.

6 Blanket stitch the bunny on green with pale yellow embroidery floss.

7 Securely sew the large yo-yo flowers with upholstery thread, where indicated on the diagram.

8 Place the pieces in rows. Using six strands of white floss, cross-stitch the pieces together. Join the rows together with cross-stitch.

9 Using wave-edge scissors, cut five strips 2½" x 36" out of White felt for the border. Use sewing thread and a small cross-stitch to join the ends of the strips together.

10 Pleat the border at the corners, and place it ½" under the edge of the throw. Use pale yellow floss, and straight stitch the border along the edge.

11 Sew a small yo-yo in each corner.

Just needle and thread, held in a caring hand, sews the gift of love in every stitch.

The Enchanted Garden

GARDEN LAP QUILT

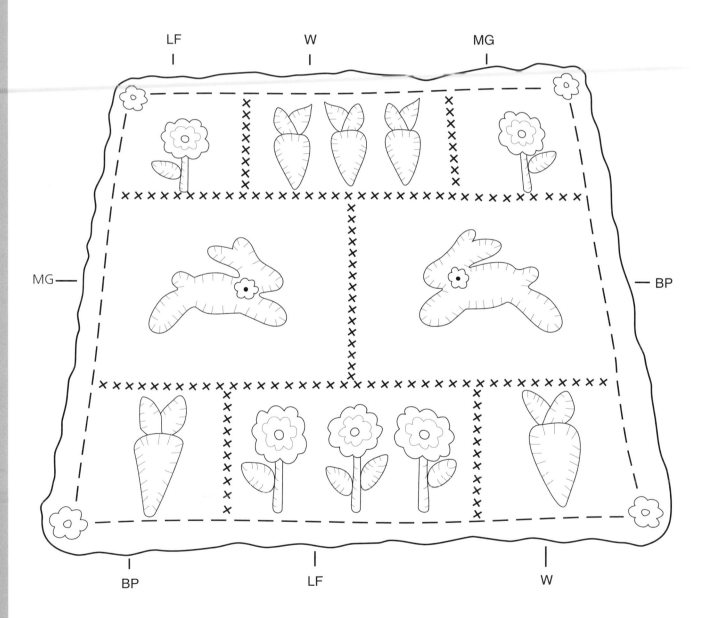

LF   W   MG

MG   BP

BP   LF   W

Braided Bunny Rug

Many nights during babyhood ARE SPENT QUICKLY LEAVING A WARM BED—THAT'S YOURS NOT THE BABY'S! THOSE CHILLY FEET DESERVE A SOFT FUZZY RUG. THIS IS A SUPER EASY PROJECT THAT USES THE STRAIGHT STITCH TO PUT IT ALL TOGETHER. IT WOULD ALSO MAKE A GREAT WALL HANGING.

SIZE: 24" LONG

- ¾ yd. Mint Green plush felt
- ¼ yd. Blush Pink plush felt
- ½ yd. White plush felt
- 9" x 12" felt pieces: 1 Leaf Green, 1 Apricot, 1 White
- Small amount of polyester fiberfill

- Embroidery floss skeins: 1 white, 1 pale green
- 3 yellow ⅜" buttons
- White upholstery thread

Tools: Wave-edge scissors, scissors, embroidery needle, sewing needle, pins, ruler, pencil.

1 Review the tips for Sewing with Plush Felt (page 9) and hand sewing the straight stitch (page 16). Cut the required pattern pieces from the pattern sheet.

2 Cut two strips of felt, 2" x 45", from Mint Green, Blush Pink, and White plush felt. Sew the two same color strips together to make 2" x 90" strips. Fold the strips in half, right sides out. Place one end of the strips on top of each other, and tack them together. Braid the three colors.

3 Pin the White plush bunny to the center of the Mint Green oval. Use white floss to straight stitch around the bunny, leaving an opening. Stuff slightly with polyester fiberfill, and finish stitching shut.

4 Cut three ½" wide pieces from Leaf Green felt: 8", 6", and 4" long. Cut around five leaves with scallop scissors. Following the dia-gram, pin the stems and leaves in place. Use pale green floss to straight stitch along the center of the stems. Stitch around the edges of the leaves, leaving a small opening. Stuff the leaves slightly, and finish stitching them shut.

5 Using scallop scissors, cut three 3" circles from Apricot felt, three 2½" circles from Blush Pink plush felt, and three 2" circles from White felt.

6 Stack the flower circles with the Blush Pink circles wrong side up. Using upholstery thread, sew the circles to the flower stems, and sew a button at the center.

7 Stretch the braid slightly, and hand press it flat. Join the ends neatly, and stitch them together. Pin the braid around the edge of the rug. Use upholstery thread to stitch through the back of the braid and rug edge, catching all three braid strips.

Remember to stop and smell the flowers, and most definitely follow any white rabbits you might see!

Braided Bunny Rug

28

BRAIDED BUNNY RUG

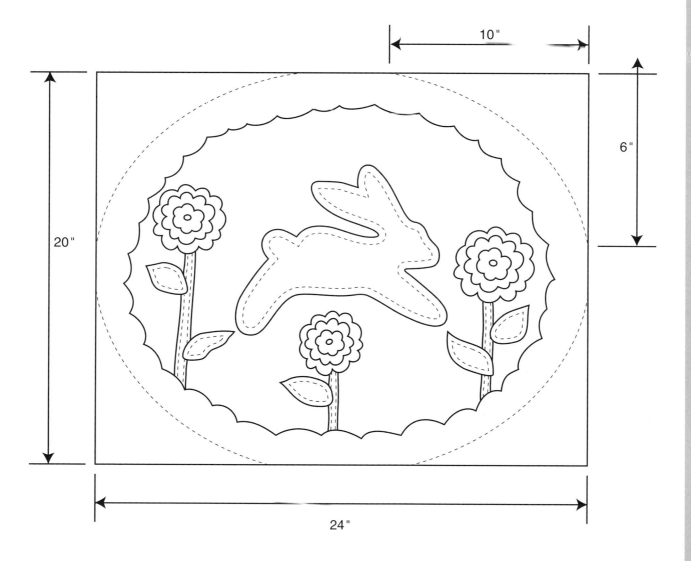

10"

6"

20"

24"

The Enchanted Garden

Ruffled Lamp

Soft lighting for those late night cozy times CAN BE EASILY CREATED WITH ANY LAMP AND SOME FABRIC. SOFT RUFFLES CAN TURN THE PLAINEST OF LAMPS INTO A CHARMING ACCESSORY.

SIZE: 24" HIGH

YOU WILL NEED:

- 1 lamp (thin, approximately 20" tall) with shade
- One 4" foam cone
- 1 yd. small floral print fabric
- 8" x 36" larger floral print fabric
- 9" x 12" piece of Apricot felt
- Seven white ½" buttons
- 3 yd. of 1½" mint green sheer wired ribbon

- White thread
- Matching threads
- 3 yd. of 32-gauge covered wire

Tools: Scissors, glue gun and low temp. glue, sewing needle, sewing machine, iron and ironing board, knife.

1 Review Covering Foam Shapes (page 10) and Creating a Yo-Yo (page 17). Cut 4" and 6" circle patterns for the yo-yos.

2 Measure the lamp shade length, and add 1½". Measure around the widest part of the lamp stem, and add 1½". This lamp required three 10" x 45" strips of the small floral print fabric—two for the stem, one for the shade—and one 6" x 36" strip to cover the base.

3 Cut six 4" circles and one 6" circle from larger floral print. Cut one 4" circle from smaller print.

4 With right sides together, sew two short sides of two 10" x 45" strips together to make a long 89½" strip. With the long sides right sides together, sew the strip into a tube. Turn and slide the tube down over the lamp stem, gathering softly as it slides on. Fasten it at the top of the lamp stem with a few stitches.

5 With right sides together, sew the base strip into a long tube for the lamp base piece. Turn. Press. Sew a gathering stitch along one side of the piece, and pull to fit around the base. Sew the ends together at the back of the base.

6 For the lamp shade, press the remaining fabric strip ½" along each long edge. Sew to create casings.

7 Measure around the bottom of the lamp shade, and cut a wire 3" longer. Repeat for the top of the lamp shade.

8 Fold the end of the wire over ½". Slide the wire through the casings, pulling it to fit around the bottom and top of the shade. Pull it snug, and the fabric should hug the shade securely. Twist the wire ends together.

9 Adjust the gathers. Overlap the ends of the fabric together at the back of the shade.

10 Sew the yo-yos. Sew buttons in the center of the smaller yo-yos. Sew one smaller yo-yo to the center of each larger yo-yo.

11 Cut five 12" pieces of mint green ribbon. Brings the ends to the middle and pinch. Sew a yo-yo at this point. Repeat for all five ribbons.

12 Evenly space yo-yos around the bottom of the shade. Glue in place.

13 Glue the other two yo-yos in place above the center ribbon yo-yo, as shown.

14 Cut the cone in half for the carrots. Cover it with Apricot felt. Cut a piece of mint greeen ribbon into three 7" pieces for each carrot.

15 Use scissors to poke a hole in the top of each carrot. Shape the ribbon pieces into loops. Glue the loops into the carrot top.

16 Glue the carrots to the lamp as desired.

It's very true that carrots do help your eyesight. Have you ever seen a bunny wearing glasses?

Flowerpot Frame

This charming frame WILL SHOWCASE ONE OF THE MANY, MANY SPECIAL PICTURES OF BABY. JUST LIKE FLOWERS, BABIES ARE SWEET AND GROW VERY FAST. THIS IS A NO SEW PROJECT TO HOLD THAT FAVORITE PICTURE.

SIZE: 16" HIGH

YOU WILL NEED:

- 9" x 12" felt pieces: 1 Apricot, 1 Leaf Green, 1 White
- 6" x 12" small floral cotton print fabric
- ⅓ yd. small check fabric
- 10" x 20" polyester quilt batt
- 2" x 4" scrap of small floral fabric
- Small amount of polyester fiberfill

- White embroidery floss
- 12" x 24" piece of cardboard

Tools: Scallop scissors, MicroTip scissors, glue gun and low temp. glue, embroidery needle, ruler, pencil.

1 Review technique for Covering Flat Cardboard Shapes (page 13). Cut the required pattern pieces from the pattern sheet.

2 Cut two cardboard pieces, one for the front and one for the back, from the pattern pieces. Flip the pattern pieces at the center to make a complete pattern. Cut an opening out of the front. On the back of the check fabric, measure and draw a line 1" from the edges of the cardboard pieces. Draw one piece ½" smaller than the cardboard. Cut out the fabric pieces.

3 Cut a piece of batting to fit the front. Glue it in place. Cut out the opening.

4 Cover the batting with a piece of check fabric. Glue it in place at the back.

5 Cut out an opening, leaving 1" all around. Make several small clips to the frame with MicroTip scissors. Turn the clips to the inside. Glue it in place.

6 Cut a 2" x 11" strip of cardboard for the frame top. Glue batting to the front of the strip. Cover it with a piece of floral fabric, and glue the overlapping edges at the back.

7 Cover the back of the frame and stand. Glue the smaller frame piece on the front of the frame back.

8 Use scallop scissors to cut two 1" x 12" strips of White felt. Glue one strip along the back of the bottom edge of the frame top. Glue another piece around the oval opening of the frame.

9 Glue the frame front to the back, leaving an opening at the top. Glue the top piece in place, extending an inch above the frame.

10 Center the frame stand on the back of the frame, keeping the bottom edges even. Glue the top of the stand to the frame.

11 Use scallop scissors to cut a 1" x 3" piece of White felt. Glue the felt between the bottom of the frame stand and the frame back. This keeps the frame upright.

12 Cut three carrots from cardboard. Glue batting to the fronts of the carrots. On the Apricot felt, measure and cut a shape ½" larger than the carrot. Cut three pieces slightly smaller.

13 Cover the front and back of each carrot.

14 Glue three Leaf Green carrot tops to the back of each carrot. Glue the carrots to the back of the frame top, evenly spaced.

15 Cut two bunnies from White felt. Sew around the edges with a small straight stitch, inserting a small amount of fiberfill before closing.

16 Cut the fabric scrap in half lengthwise. Tie the scraps around the necks of the bunnies.

17 Referring to the photo, glue the bunnies to the front of the frame.

Baby pictures, like bunnies, multiply very quickly and still we never have enough ... pictures of course!

The Enchanted Garden

Cinderbella

"Once upon a time..." EVOKES MANY FOND MEMORIES FOR ALL OF US. ONE OF THE FAVORITE STORIES MY YOUNGEST DAUGHTER ENJOYED WAS CINDERELLA. SINCE CREATING ANIMALS IS SOMETHING I LOVE TO DO, I TRANSLATED CINDERELLA INTO A SWEET BUNNY WITH A HAPPY DUCK PULLING, WHAT ELSE OF COURSE, AN EGG CARRIAGE. USING THE FOAM AND FELT TECHNIQUE AGAIN, THIS IS A DELIGHTFUL ADDITION TO THE NURSERY.

SIZE: 7" HIGH

YOU WILL NEED:

- Three 1½" foam balls
- 2" foam ball
- 6" foam egg
- 3¹⁄₁₆" x 2⁵⁄₁₆" foam egg
- 9" x 12" felt pieces: 1 Light Yellow, 1 Apricot, 1 Baby Pink, 2 Lavender
- 8" x 16" piece of Lemon Frost plush felt
- 8" square of White plush felt
- 2 black 4mm eye beads

- 2 black 5mm eye beads
- 48 pastel 6mm pearl beads
- 2 white ½" pompoms
- 1 pink ½" pompom
- 1½ yd. pastel plaid ⅜" wired ribbon

Tools: Scallop edge scissors, scissors, glue gun and low temp. glue, knife, blush, pencil, ruler, marker.

1 Review Covering Foam Shapes (page 10). Cut the required pattern pieces from the pattern sheet.

2 **For the Carriage**

a. Cut the large foam egg in half lengthwise. The narrow end is the top. On the half that is to be used as the egg front, use the pattern template to scoop out the center, ¾" deep. Cover the egg halves with Lavender felt. Use the template to cut out the center of the felt. Glue the flat sides of the egg halves together.

b. From Light Yellow felt, use scallop scissors to cut two 1" x 9" strips. Starting at the center top, glue the strip along the egg seam. Cut off the excess at the bottom. Repeat for the other half of the egg. Beginning at the bottom, glue the ribbon along the middle of the yellow felt.

c. Cut two 1½" foam balls in half for wheels. Cover the wheels with Baby Pink felt. Cut four 1" circles from Light Yellow felt. Glue them to the wheel centers on the flat side. Glue a pastel pearl in the center of each wheel.

d. Glue the wheels to the bottom of the egg, making sure they're even. Glue pearl beads in groups of three all over the egg. With scallop scissors, cut a ¾" x 8" strip from Baby Pink felt. Glue the strip around the edge of the egg opening.

e. Cover the other 1½" foam ball with White plush for the bunny head.

f. Referring to the technique on page 14, insert eye beads in the bunny face.

g. Pleat the bunny ears, and glue them to the top of the bunny head. Glue two white pompoms directly under the eyes. Glue a pink nose pompom on top of the white pompoms. Blush cheeks and ears. Glue the crown from ear to ear.

h. Insert the head into the egg opening. Glue it in place. Glue the paw under the head.

3 **For the duck**

a. Cover the small foam egg and 2" foam ball with Lemon Frost plush felt. Referring to the technique on page 14, insert the eyes. Glue the neck piece into a circle.

b. Glue the neck to the top of the wide end of the egg body. Glue the head on top of the neck. Fold the wings in half, and glue them shut. Glue the wings to either side of the duck body.

c. Glue the beak pieces together. The longer part is the upper beak. Glue the beak to the head front, directly under the eyes. Blush the cheeks.

d. From Apricot felt, cut two 1¼" x 4½" strips for the legs. Roll the strips into cylinders, and glue them to the bottom of the duck. Glue the feet pieces together, and glue them to the bottom of the legs.

4 Tie the ribbon into a bow around the duck's neck. Cut a 12" piece of ribbon for reins for the duck. Glue the end of the ribbon to the bunny paws, loop through the duck's bow, and glue it to the other side of the egg carriage.

Now off to the ball!

The Enchanted Garden

$\mathcal{B}$unny with $\mathcal{C}$hicks

After designing the bunnies in bed, I
THOUGHT ABOUT WHAT THEIR DREAMS MIGHT BE. THAT INSPIRED
A COUPLE OF SIMILAR PROJECTS. I IMAGINED THE LARGEST
BUNNY IN BED AS A MOM WHO LOVED ALL LITTLE CREATURES.
SOFT CUDDLY CHICKS SEEMED PERFECT FOR THIS FOAM AND FELT
PROJECT OF A MOM BUNNY. AROUND OUR HOME WE ALWAYS
HAVE A BABY ANIMAL, FROM ORPHAN SQUIRRELS TO KITTENS.
THERE IS ALWAYS A SOFT SPOT FOR BABIES!

SIZE: 14" TALL

Nursery Décor

- Three 2½" x 1⅞" foam eggs
- One 6" foam egg
- 3" foam ball
- 5" foam heart
- 9" x 12" felt piece: Light Yellow
- ⅓ yd. White plush felt
- 8" square Blush Pink plush felt
- 2" x 10" Mint Green plush felt
- 10" square Lemon Frost plush felt

- 4 black 4mm eye beads
- 2 black 8mm eye beads
- 2 white 1½" pompoms
- 1 pink ½" pompom
- 1 pastel ⅜" button

Tools: Wave-edge scissors, scissors, glue gun and low temp. glue, knife, blush, pencil, ruler, compass.

1 Review Covering Foam Shapes (page 10). Cut the required pattern pieces from the pattern sheet. Using the compass, draw an 8" circle pattern to cover the foam ball (bunny's head).

2 Cut all four foam eggs in half lengthwise. The narrow end is the top. Cover the four smaller egg halves, one large egg half, the foam ball, and the foam heart with White plush felt.

3 Cover the other two egg halves with Lemon Frost plush felt.

4 Cover the other large egg half with Blush Pink plush felt.

5 Referring to page 14, insert 4mm black eye beads in the chick faces and 8mm black eye beads in the bunny's face.

6 Pleat the bunny ears, and glue them to the top of the bunny's head. Glue two white pompoms directly under the eyes. Glue the pink nose pompom on top. Blush the cheeks and ears.

7 Glue the large pink and white egg halves together. Glue the heart, with the point at the back, to the bottom of the large egg. Glue the smaller white egg halves along the egg seam for arms, always flat side in.

8 Glue the head to the top of the egg. Glue the tail to the base of the body, at the back. Use the scallop scissors to cut the curved edge of the collar from Mint Green felt. Glue the collar around the neck, and glue the button in place at the center front.

9 Glue beaks to the chick faces, directly under the eyes. Overlap the edges of the wings. Glue them to either side of the body. Glue feet to the bottom of the chicks. Glue the chicks to the large bunny, as shown.

More Thoughts

CREATE ONE LITTLE CHICK AND BRIGHTEN SOMEONE'S DAY WITH A FLUFF OF SUNSHINE.

The Enchanted Garden

Flower Memo Holder

Special moments with babies HAPPEN EVERY DAY. THEY GROW SO FAST WE WANT TO CAPTURE IT ALL. THE MEMO BOARD CAN LOVINGLY DISPLAY THIS WEEK'S FAVORITE PHOTOS AS WELL AS IMPORTANT NOTES FOR APPOINTMENTS OR A CUTE MOMENT WITH BABY. THE POCKETS CAN HOLD EXTRA PICTURES, NOTEPAPER, OR LITTLE BABY NECESSITIES.

SIZE: 30" HIGH

YOU WILL NEED:

- 12" x 16½" x 1" foam board
- 12" x 16" piece of lightweight cardboard
- 14" x 45" small floral print fabric
- 1 yd. of a coordinating larger floral print
- 9" x 12" felt piece: 1 Apricot, 1 Leaf Green
- ⅔ yd. White felt
- 7 white ½" buttons
- White upholstery thread

- Matching threads
- 2 sheets PeelnStick™ double-sided adhesive

Tools: Wave-edge scissors, scissors, glue gun and low temp. glue, sewing needle, sewing machine, tacky fabric glue, iron and ironing board, pencil, ruler.

1 Review the techniques for Covering Flat Foam Shapes (page 12) and Creating a Yo-Yo (page 17). Cut the required pattern pieces from the pattern sheet. Cut 4" and 6" circle patterns for the yo-yos. Glue a cardboard piece to the back of the foam board. Glue a piece of White felt to cover the front of the foam top.

2 From the larger floral print, cut two 7½" strips for the ruffle, one 11½" x 45" strip for the pocket, and seven 4" circles and two 6" circles for the yo-yos. From the smaller floral print, cut a 14" x 21" piece, and two 3½" x 16" pieces for straps.

3 Using wave-edge scissors for one edge, cut two 2½" x 36" strips and one 2½" x 18" strip from White felt. Cut three ½" x 36" strips using wave-edge scissors.

4 Cut the remaining pattern pieces from felt.

5 Using the techniques for Covering Foam Shapes, cover the front of the foam board with a small floral print.

6 Sew the fabric and felt ruffle strips together, making 90" long ruffle pieces.

7 Press the long fabric strip in half, right sides out.

8 Place the felt ruffle on top of the fabric ruffle, matching the bottom edges. Gather it together along the bottom edge, and pull to fit it around three sides of the board.

9 Place the ½" strips diagonally across the board front, as shown. Glue the ends over the back of the board.

10 Glue the ruffle along the back edge of the board.

11 Press the edges of the straps in ¼". Fold them in half lengthwise, press, and topstitch.

12 With right sides together, press the pocket piece in half. Sew around the pocket with a ¼" seam, leaving a small opening. Turn right sides out, and press.

13 Fold the pocket piece up 4" lengthwise, and press. Divide the pocket evenly into three pocket sections, and topstitch.

14 Using the adhesive sheets according to the manufacturer's instructions, adhere the bunnies to the pockets. Attach the three carrots to the center pocket.

15 Glue the pocket along the bottom of the memo board.

16 Measure in 2" from the top of the board on either side. Glue the straps in place, extending them 8" above the board.

17 Cover the back of the board with a piece of White felt.

18 Sew the yo-yos. Sew the buttons in the center of the smaller yo-yos. Sew two smaller yo-yos to the center of the larger yo-yos.

19 Use glue to fasten the yo-yos on the front of the board where the felt strips intersect.

20 Sew the large yo-yos to the ends of the straps, and make a loop at the back of the straps at the same time to hang the board.

May the memories of these special times remain in your heart always.

The Enchanted Garden

Baby Flops Bunny

Every baby needs a cuddly friend just their size. BABY FLOPS HAS JUST LEARNED TO SIT UP AND IS SO SURPRISED. BOTH OF MY DAUGHTERS HAVE THEIR FAVORITE SOFT FRIENDS WHO HAVE BEEN CHERISHED AND LOVED FOR YEARS, FULL OF PATCHES UPON PATCHES. BABY FLOPS WITH HER SOFT FUZZY BODY, APPLIQUÉD FEATURES, AND SAFETY EYES IS THE PERFECT COMPANION FOR ANY BABY. SEW EASY AND SO SWEET.

SIZE: 14" SITTING

- ¾ yd. Lemon Frost plush felt
- 12" x 20" Blush Pink plush felt
- 2" square Victorian Rose plush felt
- 16 oz. polyester fiberfill
- 2 black 8mm safety eyes
- 1 skein pale green embroidery floss
- Matching threads

Tools: Scissors, sewing machine, embroidery needle, measuring tape, pins, pencil, marker.

1 Review the tips for Sewing With Plush Felt (page 9) and hand sewing the blanket stitch (page 16). Cut the required pattern pieces from the pattern sheet. The seams are ¼", double stitched. The plush pieces are sewn right sides together.

2 Pin the leg pieces to the front and back of the body, and sew.

3 Refer to page 14 for the eye technique. Slit the center front body. Make small holes in the face for eyes. Insert the eyes, and secure the backs in place.

4 Pin the face features in place, and blanket stitch. At the nose point, make a straight 1½" stitch for the mouth.

5 Align the front and back body pieces, and sew. Clip the curves. Turn the body through the front slit. Stuff the feet and paws firmly. Stuff the arms and legs softly. There should be no fiberfill where the arms and legs bend. Stuff the head firmly and the body softly. As the body is stuffed, the slit will widen to give bunny a rounder tummy.

6 Pin the hearts to the feet, and blanket stitch. Pin the tummy piece centered over the slit, and blanket stitch.

7 Sew the ear lining to the outer ear. Tightly gather the ends of the ears. Matching Xs, securely sew in place. Bring the paw up to the mouth, and sew.

How many carrots in a carrot patch? Never enough, according to a bunny. Though we all know too many stuffed carrots can lead to overstuffed bunnies.

The Enchanted Garden

Stuffed Carrot

One year my daughter, AMANDA, DRESSED AS A LARGE BLACK AND WHITE BUNNY (COURTESY OF AN OLD WINTER COAT) FOR HALLOWEEN. WE OFTEN HAVE SNOW FOR HALLOWEEN, SO COSTUMES MUST BE WARM. I ALSO MADE HER A VERY LARGE CARROT TO CARRY UNDER HER ARM. EVER SINCE THEN I HAVE ENJOYED GIVING ALL MY BUNNIES STUFFED CARROTS.

SIZE: 13" LONG

YOU WILL NEED:

- 9" x 12" felt pieces: 2 Leaf Green, 1 Apricot
- Small amount of polyester fiberfill
- 2 white chenille stems
- White upholstery thread

Tools: Wave-edge scissors, scissors, glue gun and low temp. glue, sewing needle, pins, pencil.

1 Cut the required pattern pieces from the pattern sheet.

2 Cut two carrot pieces from Apricot felt. Align the pieces, and sew them together.

3 Turn the right side out, and stuff firmly

4 Use wave-edge scissors to cut six leaves from Leaf Green felt. Cut three 6" pieces from chenille stems.

5 Start at the bottom of a leaf, and lay a chenille stem along the center of the leaf. Glue another leaf on top, sandwiching the chenille stem. Repeat for all leaves.

6 Insert leaves 1" into the top of the carrot. Using upholstery thread, sew the leaves in place.

More Thoughts

MAKE A BUNCH OF CARROTS FOR A MOBILE OR FILL A WICKER BASKET. WHO KNOWS WHEN A HUNGRY BUNNY MIGHT NEED A SNACK.

Notes

Nurture your dreams

Nursery Décor

Chapter 3
Boys, Bears, and Baseball

In my neighborhood, there is the sweetest baby boy, all smiles and blonde hair. Several of his little baseball outfits and sneakers helped accessorize this room. I thought of him as I put it together—pulling the wagon, hugging the puppy, or throwing the ball pillows. This room is for all the tiny sports fans out there whose proud dads bring home gloves, bats, and balls before they're even sitting up.

Benjamin Bear

For a hundred years, BEARS HAVE BEEN A CHERISHED COMPANION FOR CHILDREN. THEIR LOVING EXPRESSIONS AND CUDDLY BODIES SEEM TO SAY "HUG ME." MY DAUGHTER AMANDA'S FAVORITE BEAR, "TEDDY," STILL SITS IN HER ROOM AFTER TWENTY YEARS. WITH MATTED FUR, SEVERAL BARE SPOTS, AND REPLACED EARS, HE HAS BEEN WELL LOVED. THIS EASY BEAR, BENJAMIN, WITH A ONE-PIECE BODY IS BOTH CUTE AND CUDDLY. HE WOULD BE A LOVING COMPANION FOR ANY LITTLE BABY BOY AND STURDY ENOUGH TO FOLLOW HIM THROUGH MANY CHILDHOOD ADVENTURES.

SIZE: 16" SITTING

YOU WILL NEED:

- 2/3 yd. tan curly synthetic fur (54"–60" wide)
- Two 12mm safety eyes
- 6 oz. polyester fiberfill
- 1 skein brown embroidery floss
- Matching threads

Tools: Sharp scissors, sewing machine, embroidery needle, needle, pins, marker.

1 Cut out the required pattern pieces from the pattern sheet. Have the nap of the fur running down for the bear. On the wrong side of the fur, draw the pattern pieces. When cutting out the pieces, cut through the backing only.

2 Align the pieces with right sides together. Pin the seams together, tucking the fur inside. Sew them with ¼" seams. Double stitch all seams. Clip the curves. Turn right side out.

3 For the head, sew the fronts together at the center seam. Pin the back to the front, matching the letters. Sew from A to B. Clip the curves. Turn right side out. Fluff the fur along the seams by running a needle along them and pulling out any caught pieces.

4 Referring to page 14, insert safety eyes according to the marks on the head pattern piece.

5 Stuff the head with fiberfill, stuffing the nose very firmly. Sew a gathering stitch around the bottom of the head; pull the threads tight. Secure the thread.

6 Trim the fur close to the backing in the nose area. With three strands of embroidery floss, satin stitch the nose. Use the diagram as a guide. Don't cut the thread.

7 For the mouth, use the last stitch of the nose at the bottom point. Bring the needle out and make a ½" straight stitch down the center seam. Bring the needle out ½" to each side, back to the center, and out through the bottom of the head to secure the thread.

8 Sew each pair of ear pieces together along the curved edge. Turn. Stitch the raw bottom edges together. Refer to the pattern piece for ear placement. Pin and stitch the bottom of the ears in place.

9 Sew the body front and back together, leaving an opening where indicated. Turn. Stuff the paws and feet very firmly to the line indicated on the body pattern piece. Stuff the remainder of the legs and arms softly. Stuff the body firmly enough that it will spring back when squeezed. Sew a gathering stitch around the neck. Pull the threads tight, and secure.

10 To attach the head to the body, refer to the diagram. Lightly draw a 2" circle at the center of the bottom of the head. Use needle and thread to secure the head to the center of the neck gathers on the body. Take the needle through the edge of the circle on the bottom of the head back through the neck. Keep the stitches loose, taking the needle back and forth around the circle. Pull the stitches very tight at the end of the circle. Secure the thread at the neck.

11 To dress your bear, choose a baby shirt that's approximately a size 18 months.

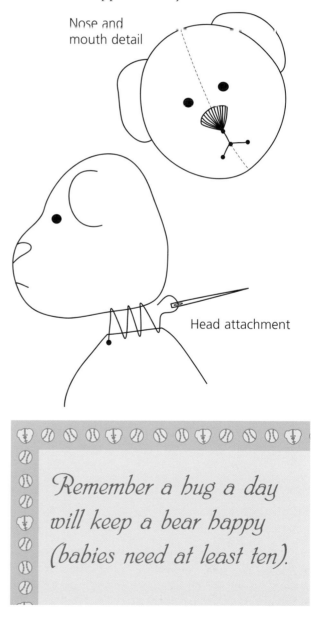

Nose and mouth detail

Head attachment

Remember a hug a day will keep a bear happy (babies need at least ten).

Baseball Throw

Every baby's room needs a fleecy blanket. THERE
ARE SO MANY TIMES A COZY COVER IS NEEDED. LAY IT ON THE FLOOR
SO BABY CAN PLAY, USE IT AS A STROLLER OR CARRIAGE BLANKET, AND
CUDDLE UP WITH BABY AND A BOOK AT BEDTIME. THIS THROW IS A
FUN PROJECT FOR THE LITTLEST OF BOY'S ROOMS.

SIZE: 46" SQUARE

YOU WILL NEED:

- 1 1/4 yd. denim Berber fleece
- 9" x 12" felt pieces: 3 Antique White
- 1/3 yd. plaid flannel in both red and blue
- 2 skeins red embroidery floss
- 6 oz. polyester fiberfill
- Matching threads

Tools: Scissors, sewing machine, embroidery needle, pins, invisible marker, iron and ironing board.

1 Cut the required pattern piece from the pattern sheet. Cut 12 baseballs from felt. Use a marker to draw lines on each ball.

2 Refer back to page 16 for the cross-stitch technique. Using six strands of red embroidery floss, stitch ⅜" wide cross-stitches on all lines on the baseballs. (**Note:** *Use fabric marker or paint for a quick stitch finish.*)

3 Cut the plaid flannel into two 5" x 45" strips for each color. Press the strips in half lengthwise. With right sides together, pin strips of one color to opposite sides of the fleece square. Sew with a ⅝" seam. Trim.

4 Lay the remaining strips along the remaining sides. Turn in the ends of the strips even with the edges of the adjoining strips. Press the ends and stitch shut. With right sides together, pin the strips to the sides. Sew, and trim seams.

5 Topstitch the flannel sides close to the inner edge of the blanket, all around the throw.

6 Pin baseballs to the front of the throw in a random pattern. Refer to the diagram. It should look like the balls were thrown on the fleece.

7 Topstitch around the edge of each ball, leaving a small opening. Stuff the balls slightly to give a dimensional look. Finish topstitching closed. Repeat for all balls.

Appliqué Pattern Guide

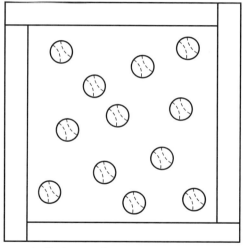

Baseball Throw Placemat

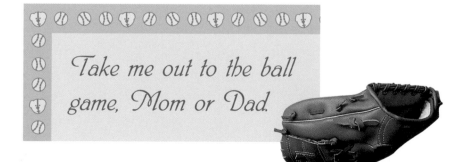

Take me out to the ball game, Mom or Dad.

Boys, Bears, and Baseball

Waggles the Puppy

Before he is old enough to ask for one, MAKE THIS ADORABLE PUPPY FOR YOUR LITTLE GUY. SIT WAGGLES WHERE BABY CAN SEE HIM, AND HE WILL SMILE WITH DELIGHT. (SO WILL WAGGLES!)

SIZE: 8" LONG

YOU WILL NEED:

- 1/6 yd. tan curly synthetic fur
- 1/6 yd. brown curly synthetic fur
- 1" x 10" denim blue felt
- 8 oz. polyester fiberfill
- Two 6mm safety eyes
- 1/2" brown pompom
- 8 oz. plastic doll pellets, optional
- Matching threads
- Upholstery thread

Tools: Scissors, sewing machine, needle, pins, marker.

1 Cut out the required pattern pieces from the pattern sheet. Draw the pattern pieces on the back of the fur. Cut the pieces out of the fur, being careful to cut through only the backing.

2 Sew all the pieces, except the head, right sides together with a ⅛" seam. Double sew all of the seams. Leave openings where indicated. Before sewing the top and underbody together, insert the tail and sew it in the opening. Turn all pieces.

3 Fill the feet halfway with pellets or polyester fiberfill. Use upholstery thread to securely stitch the legs in place.

4 Stuff the body lightly. Gather around the neck edge, pull stitches tight, and secure the thread.

5 Referring to page 14, insert safety eyes into the front of the face at the dots. Use upholstery thread to securely sew a pompom nose in place. (A safety nose or embroidered nose should be used if you're giving this to baby to play with.) Slit the back of the head piece. Sew the head pieces right sides together. Turn. Sew the slit opening shut.

6 Gather the ends of the ears tight. Secure the threads. Pin the ears in place on the head, and sew securely.

7 Pin the head to the gathered neck edge. With small stitches, sew the back of the head to the neck in a small 1" circle.

8 Place the felt collar around the neck, and stitch in place.

Waggles is such a good puppy, already paper-trained and with an A+ from obedience school.

Baseball Toy Holder

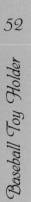

Little guys always have all KINDS OF FUN STUFF. THIS TOY HOLDER MAKES BOTH A GREAT PLACE FOR STORING BABY THINGS AS WELL AS AN ATTRACTIVE WALL HANGING. THE BRIGHT COLORS WILL DELIGHT BABY, TOO.

SIZE: 14" x 42"

YOU WILL NEED:

- 1 yd. denim blue felt
- 9" x 12" felt pieces: 2 Sandstone, 2 White, 2 Red
- ⅛ yd. fusible web
- Red thread
- 15" of ½" dowel
- Matching threads

Tools: Scissors, sewing machine, iron and ironing board, pins, marker, ruler.

Nursery Décor

1 Cut the required pattern pieces from the pattern sheet. Cut out baseballs and bats from felt.

2 From denim felt, cut five tabs 2" x 6" and two pieces 14" x 30".

3 Cut the Red 9" x 12" pieces in half lengthwise. Cut one half-piece in half again, from one upper corner to the opposite lower corner to make two triangles for the bottom of the toy holder. Cut one White piece of felt in half, and cut that half into triangles as done for the red triangles.

4 Referring to the diagram, pin the triangles to the bottom of the back piece of the toy holder. Overlap the tops of the triangles, keeping the bottoms even. Trim off some of the triangle tops, if necessary.

5 Fold the denim tabs in half, and pin them evenly along the top. Align the top piece of the toy holder over the bottom. Pin it in place. With red thread, top stitch in at ¼" completely around the piece.

6 Using red thread and a small zigzag stitch, sew lines on the baseballs.

7 Refer to the manufacturer's instructions to fuse the bats and balls to the red pocket pieces.

8 Following the diagram, pin the pockets to the toy holder, topstitch with red thread.

9 Place the dowel through the top to hang. You can paint the dowel, or hang it, as shown in the room, with a bat and ball over the top. (See page 62 to make the bat and ball.)

What are little boys made of? Smiles and hugs, just watch out for the hidden bugs!

More Thoughts

MAKE TWO TO HANG ON EITHER SIDE OF THE CHANGE TABLE TO HOLD HANDY ITEMS. HANG ONE ON THE DOOR, AND PLACE CURRENT PICTURES IN THE POCKETS. THAT WAY YOU CAN SHOW THEM OFF EVEN WHEN BABY IS SLEEPING.

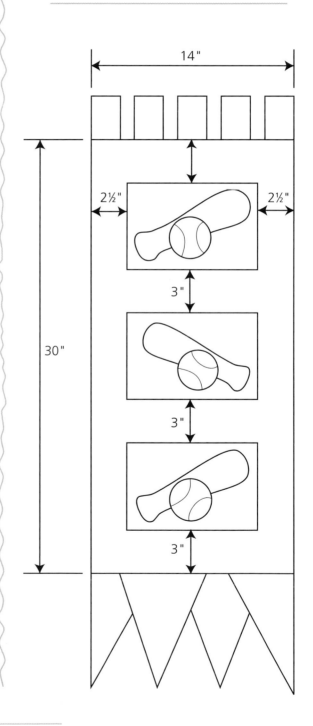

Sports Pillows

When both of my daughters were babies, I LOVED
MAKING ALL KINDS OF PILLOWS WITH DIFFERENT DESIGNS AND SHAPES.
I USED THEM TO DECORATE THE ROOM, IN ROCKERS, ON THE FLOOR,
AND ON SHELVES. I WOULD PILE THEM TO LEAN AGAINST, SINCE MUCH
OF MY TIME SEEMED SPENT ON THE FLOOR. LIFE HAS A DIFFERENT
PERSPECTIVE ON THE FLOOR.

SIZE: 14" SQUARE

YOU WILL NEED:

- 1 yd. Navy felt
- 9" x 12" felt pieces: 2 Red, 2 White
- Two 14" pillow forms
- Red, white embroidery floss
- 1/3 yd. fusible web
- Matching threads

Tools: Scissors, sewing machine, embroidery needle, pins, invisible marker, ruler.

1 Review the outline stitch (page 16) and the Simple Pillow Style (page 18).

2 Cut the required pattern pieces from the pattern sheet.

3 Cut two 15" square pillow fronts from Navy felt. Cut two 16" square backs, and cut them each in half.

4 Trim the Red and White pieces into 9" squares.

5 Trace the bat on the Red felt at an angle. Using three strands of white embroidery floss, outline the bat. Repeat with the ball on White felt, using red embroidery floss.

6 For each pillow, angle a corresponding Red or White square as a baseball diamond. Following the manufacturer's directions, fuse the square to a Navy pillow front. Topstitch in place.

7 Fuse the embroidered squares over the top of the diamonds, as shown in the picture. Topstitch in place.

8 Overlap the two pillow back pieces by 1". Pin the ends to hold. Sew the front to the back with a ¼" seam. Turn, and fit in the pillow forms.

More Thoughts

THESE PILLOWS WOULD BE A FUN BIRTHDAY GIFT WITH THE AGE NUMBER EMBROIDERED IN THE CORNERS OF THE DIAMOND.

Boys, Bears, and Baseball

Tiny Teddy

I have a weakness for teddy bears. MY OFFICE AND STUDIO RESEMBLE DENS WITH BEARS HERE AND THERE ON SHELVES AND FILING CABINETS, WHEREVER THERE IS A LITTLE SPACE TO PLACE ONE. LUCKILY THIS FURRY FELLOW CAN FIT ALMOST ANYWHERE.

SIZE: 8"

- 18" x 22" piece Brown Sugar craft cut shaggy plush felt
- 5" x 14" knit or Polarfleece®
- 6 oz. polyester fiberfill
- 2 black 5mm eye beads
- Black embroidery floss

- Matching threads
- Upholstery thread
- ¾" wood heart and barn red paint (optional)

Tools: Scissors, sewing machine, embroidery needle, needle, black fine-tip marker.

1 Cut the required pattern pieces from the pattern sheet. Draw the pattern pieces on the wrong side of the shaggy felt, and cut them out. Cut out the sweater.

2 Sew the body and leg pieces with right sides together. Clip the curves, and turn.

3 Gather around the edge of the muzzle, pull stitches tight, and secure threads.

4 Refer to the muzzle pattern piece for the nose and mouth placement. With three strands of black embroidery floss, embroider the nose with straight stitches. Stitch down from the nose point ¼" and stitch ⅛" to each side of the straight stitch.

5 Stuff the body and legs firmly. Turn the lower edge of the body under ½". Center the leg seams. Insert the legs ½" into the bottom of the body edge. With upholstery thread, top-stitch the legs securely in place.

6 With upholstery thread, anchor the thread at the back of the neck. Take the needle up and through the neck to the eye mark. Slide a bead on the needle. Take the needle through to the opposite eye mark, and place a bead on the needle. Return the needle to the back of the neck. Pull the thread to indent the beads slightly. Take several stitches to secure the thread.

7 Return the needle to the front of the face. Place the muzzle in position, and securely stitch around the edge of the muzzle. Return the needle to the back of the neck.

8 Sew the sweater seams. Turn the neck, sleeves, and bottom under ¼". Topstitch. Place the sweater on the bear.

9 If desired, paint the wood heart with a barn red color, and glue it to the sweater. (This isn't recommended if baby will be playing with this teddy.)

More thoughts

STENCIL OR PAINT A HEART ON TEDDY'S SWEATER TO MAKE IT A BABY PROOF TOY. EMBROIDER A HEART OR INITIAL WITH EMBROIDERY FLOSS.

MAKE A FEW LITTLE TEDDIES TO CREATE A MOBILE TO HANG OVER THE CRIB. HANG THEM BY THEIR PAWS OR BODY SO THEY TWIRL, DOING ALL KINDS OF TRICKS.

How many teddy bears are too many? Don't ask me, I've lost count at my house!

Diaper Stacker

This is such a simple and PRACTICAL PROJECT WITH A GREAT LOOK. A DIAPER STACKER IS HANDY HUNG RIGHT NEXT TO A CHANGE TABLE. USUALLY ONE HAND IS TOTALLY OCCUPIED HANGING ONTO A SQUIRMING BUNDLE, SO ONE QUICK REACH WITH THE OTHER FOR A DIAPER IS ALL THAT'S REQUIRED. ONE DAY I LET GO OF MY DAUGHTER AMANDA FOR A SECOND, DURING WHICH SHE SHOT HERSELF OFF THE TABLE. SHE HAD HER FEET AGAINST THE SIDE WITH BENT KNEES AND GAVE A BIG KICK. NEEDLESS TO SAY, I NEVER LET GO AGAIN.

SIZE: 11" x 25"

YOU WILL NEED:

- 72" x 3/4 yd. Navy felt
- 9" x 12" felt pieces: 2 White, 1 Red
- 12" square of fusible web
- 1 skein red Needleloft craft cord
- Red thread
- 10" of 3/8" dowel
- 10" square of heavy cardboard
- Matching threads

Tools: Scissors, sewing machine, iron and ironing board, pins, invisible marker.

1 Cut the required pattern pieces from the pattern sheet. Cut out the balls and bat from felt. Following the manufacturer's directions, apply fusible web to the balls and bat.

2 Draw stitch lines on the fronts of the balls. With red thread, topstitch the stitch lines on the balls, and topstitch around the outside edge of the balls.

3 With red thread, topstitch around the outside edge of the bat.

4 From Navy felt, cut two pieces 22" x 26" and one piece 22" x 12". With right sides together and a ½" seam, sew a long strip along each 22" side of the short strip. With the seams on the inside, fold the piece in half to make it 11" wide. Press. Topstitch along the folded edge. This is the front of the diaper stacker.

5 Topstitch the back edges of the diaper stacker together along the long sides, leaving the bottom open. Cardboard will slide in between the layers to create a solid bottom.

6 Bring the two top ends together. Sew along the edge. Measure down ½", and sew along this line to make a pocket for the dowel. Turn this pocket to the inside of the diaper stacker.

7 With a few small stitches at the back of the balls and bat, sew them to the diaper stacker corners and top.

8 Decide how high the diaper stacker will be hung. Cut a piece of craft cord twice the length required.

9 Fold the craft cord in half. Stitch the middle of the cord securely to the center top of the diaper stacker. Tie and knot the ends. Slide in the dowel and cardboard. Hang the diaper stacker from the ceiling.

More thoughts

APPLIQUÉ THE BALL AND BAT TO A FELT WINDOW CURTAIN.

Boys, Bears, and Baseball

Once babies are sitting up, THEY ENJOY PICKING UP TOYS AND THROWING THEM. FOR A TINY BUDDING BASEBALL PLAYER, THESE BALL PILLOWS ARE FUN. SOFT TO ROLL ON, THROW, AND TOSS, THESE PILLOWS ARE GREAT FOR BABY AND PARENT. MAKE DIFFERENT SIZES FOR YOUR LITTLE BALLPLAYER.

SIZE: 8", 10"

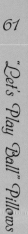

YOU WILL NEED:

- 1/3 yd. White plush felt
- 8 oz. polyester fiberfill
- 1 yd. Needleloft red craft cord
- Red thread
- Matching threads

Tools: Scissors, sewing machine, needle, compass, pencil, pins.

1 Using the compass (or an appropriate size plate), draw two 11" and two 9" circles on the wrong side of the plush. Cut out.

2 To mark the line for the cord, place the edge of the back piece of plush over the front piece by a third. Follow this curved inner edge for the line of the cord. Pin in place. Repeat for the opposite side of the front. The lines should be approximately 3" apart at the center.

3 Repeat for the second ball. There should be approximately 2" between the lines at the center of the front.

4 With a small zigzag stitch, topstitch the cord to the front of the balls.

5 Cut a 3" slit in the center of each back.

6 With right sides together, sew the fronts to the backs with ¼" seams. Turn.

7 Stuff the balls, pushing the fiberfill to the edges. Fill the middle in last. Sew the back slit shut, and secure the threads.

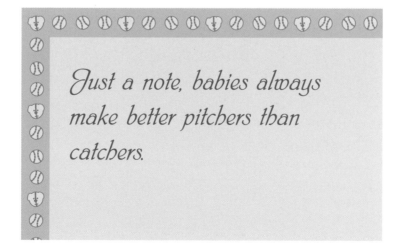

Just a note, babies always make better pitchers than catchers.

Bat and Ball

For the serious coach AND HIS "LITTLE LEAGUER," THIS IS
A GREAT FIRST BAT AND BALL. USE IT AS A DECORATIVE ACCENT, OR,
FOR THE LITTLE GUY WHO'S SITTING UP, USE IT AS A FUN TOY. IT'S
SAFE TO SWING (AND HIT) AT ANYTHING AT ALL, AND IT MAKES A
DELIGHTFUL SHOWER GIFT FOR A PROUD SPORTS DAD.

SIZE: 22" LONG

YOU WILL NEED:

- ⅛ yd. Light Heather Brown plush
- 6" x 12" white plush
- 16 oz. polyester fiberfill
- ½ yd. Needleloft red craft cord
- Red thread
- Matching threads

Tools: Scissors, sewing machine, needle, pins, invisible marker.

1 Cut the required pattern pieces from the pattern sheet. Cut the bat and ball out of felt.

2 Slit the center of the back of the ball. Draw lines for the ball stitching on the front of the ball. Cut the craft cord in half. With a small zigzag stitch, sew the craft cord along the lines. Trim off the excess.

3 With right sides together, sew around the bat and ball. Turn. Stuff firmly.

4 Stitch the openings shut. If the bat and ball will be used as a wall hanging, sew the ball to the front of the bat. Sew thread loops at either end of the bat to hang.

Let's play ball!

Notes

Always play

Nursery Décor

Chapter 4

Sail Away on a Sea of Stars

This cheery room is filled with bright colors and fanciful projects. Delightful baby animals sail away in an ark and matching wall hanging. A sleepy mouse drifts along on a starry mobile. Endearing and imaginative, this room is perfect for baby's sweet dreams.

"My Little Star" Frame

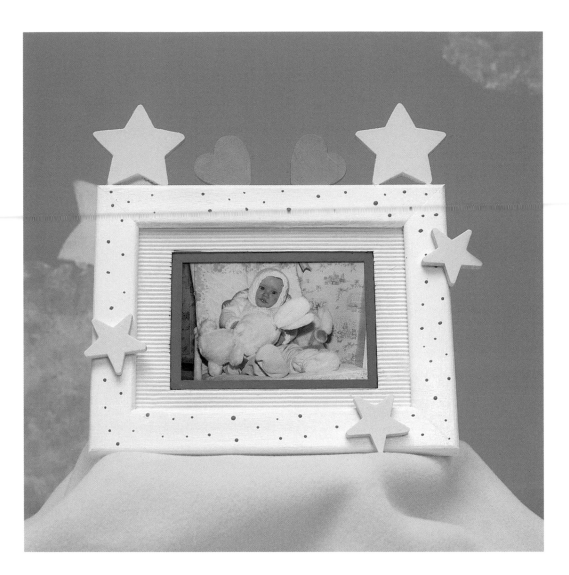

The first month my daughter was home I WENT THROUGH A ROLL OF FILM A WEEK. EVERY MOVE AND FACIAL EXPRESSION WAS AMAZING TO ME. THE MAGIC OF PHOTOGRAPHY LETS US CAPTURE THOSE SPECIAL MOMENTS AND REMEMBER THEM LOVINGLY. PICTURE FRAMES CAN BE DECORATED TO COORDINATE WITH AND HIGHLIGHT THOSE SPECIAL PHOTOS. HEARTS AND STARS WITH A LITTLE PAINT CREATE A LOVELY ACCENT FOR YOUR BABY'S ROOM.

SIZE: 7" x 9"

Nursery Décor

YOU WILL NEED:

- 7" x 9" (outside measurement) picture frame with 5" x 7" mat (or purchase the mat separately)
- Two 1½" wood hearts
- Three 1½" wood stars
- Two 2½" wood stars
- DecoArt Crafter's Acrylic: Luscious Lemon, Cool Blue, White
- DecoArt DuraClear satin varnish
- Wood glue

Tools: Small foam brush, palette or plastic lid.

1 Remove the glass from the frame. Squeeze small amounts of paint onto the palette.

2 Paint the inside mat of the frame with Luscious Lemon and Cool Blue.

3 Paint the frame White, stars Luscious Lemon, and hearts Cool Blue. Use two coats.

4 To create dots, dip the end of the brush into Cool Blue paint and press it to the frame.

5 Let dry. Apply two coats of varnish. Glue the wood hearts and 2½" wood stars to the top of the frame.

6 Glue the 1½" wood stars to the sides of the frame.

7 Place the glass back in the frame. Add a special photo.

A picture is worth not only a thousand words but more than a thousand remembrances.

Sail Away on a Sea of Stars

Gentle Giraffe

One of the great things about having a baby IS IT GIVES US AN EXCUSE TO SURROUND OURSELVES WITH SOFT CUDDLY ANIMALS. THEY ALWAYS BRING A SMILE AND EVEN BIGGER SMILES WHEN SHARING THEM WITH BABY. IT'S FUN TO BRING A CUTE ANIMAL TO LIFE WITH SOUNDS AND MOVEMENT, ESPECIALLY WHEN YOUR AUDIENCE IS COOING AND GRINNING. YOUR ACTING SKILLS WILL WIN YOU AN OSCAR EVERY TIME WITH YOUR BABY. THIS GENTLE GIRAFFE WILL GIVE YOU AND BABY MANY HOURS OF IMAGINATIVE FUN.

SIZE: 18" TALL

- ½ yd. Cashmere Tan plush felt
- 9" x 12" felt pieces: 2 Walnut Brown
- 16 oz. polyester fiberfill
- 2 black 8mm safety eyes
- Tan upholstery thread
- Matching threads

Tools: Scissors, sewing machine, pins, needle, brown fine-tip marker.

1 Review Animal Features on page 14.

2 Cut the required pattern pieces from the pattern sheet. Cut the pieces from plush and felt, including a tail 3½" x 4½" from the plush.

3 With right sides together, leaving openings as indicated, sew around the body, ears, legs, and hooves.

4 Turn the pieces right sides out. Insert eyes at the marks indicated on the pattern piece. Stuff the head firmly and continue to fill the rest of the body. Stitch the opening shut.

5 Stuff the legs firmly. Slide a hoof over the end of each leg, matching the back seams. With upholstery thread, stitch along the top edge of the hoof. Repeat for the other legs.

6 Place the open top of the legs in position at the bottom of the body. With upholstery thread, stitch around the top of the leg, securely attaching it to the body. (Make a small stitch in the leg, through the body layer, and back through the leg all the way around. Secure the thread. Repeat for all legs.)

7 Stitch the bottom of the ears shut. Place the ears in position on the head, and sew them in place.

8 With the wrong sides together, stitch the horn pieces around the edges. Sew them in place between the ears.

9 Cut fringe on the tail strip ½" along the 3½" side. Roll the tail into a 1" diameter tube, and stitch the edge. Place it in position on the giraffe. Sew in place.

10 Place the nose pieces, and arrange the spots randomly on the body. Stitch around the edges on all pieces.

More Thoughts

IF YOU'RE SHORT ON TIME, USE FABRI-TAC™ TO GLUE THE SPOTS IN PLACE. IT'S VERY IMPORTANT TO MAKE SURE THE SPOTS ARE SECURE, BECAUSE NO SELF-RESPECTING GIRAFFE WOULD BE SEEN WITHOUT HIS SPOTS!

A favorite book, comfy rocker, AND CUDDLY BABY ARE A PERFECT COMBINATION. THIS UNIQUE BOOK HOLDER IS THE PLACE TO KEEP THOSE WELL-LOVED BOOKS. THERE ARE ALWAYS A FEW BOOKS THAT ARE READ OVER AND OVER AGAIN.

SIZE: 16" HIGH

- 2" foam ball
- 2⁵⁄₁₆" x 3" foam egg
- Two 1" x 1¹⁵⁄₁₆" foam eggs
- ¼ yd. White plush felt
- 9" x 12" felt pieces: 1 Light Yellow, 1 Misty Blue, 1 White
- 2 black 6mm eye beads
- 2 white 1" pompoms
- 1 yellow ½" pompom
- 1 black ½" pompom
- 1½" wood star

- DecoArt Crafter's Acrylic: Luscious Lemon, Cool Blue
- DecoArt DuraClear satin varnish
- 10" star papier-mâché box
- 1¼ yd. Wrights® rainbow rickrack
- Plaid® Monogram Forum Classic 1½" stencil

Tools: Microtip scissors, glue gun and low temp. glue sticks, 2" foam brush, ¼" stencil brush, pins, knife, blush.

1 Review Covering Foam Shapes on page 10. Cut the required pattern pieces from the pattern sheet. Cut the pieces from plush and felt.

2 Cut a thin slice off the foam ball (head). Cut a thin slice off the bottom of the 2⁵⁄₁₆ x 3" foam egg (body). Cut one smaller foam egg in half lengthwise (bottom feet). Cut a third off each long side of the other small egg (front paws).

3 From White plush, cut a 5" circle for the head and a 7" circle for the body. Cut ovals for the egg shapes 2" larger than the shape, and ovals the same size to cover the bottoms of the feet and paws.

4 Cover all foam pieces, top and bottoms.

5 On the front of the face, make small holes for the eyes, ⅜" apart. Glue the black eye beads in place. Glue two white pompoms side by side underneath the eyes. Glue the black pom-pom nose on top.

6 Pleat the ear and glue the bottom edges. Glue the ear to one side of the head, above the eyes. Blush the cheeks and ear.

7 Glue the bottom of the head to the narrow end of the egg body. Angle back the feet, and glue under the bottom end. Angle the front paws out, and glue them to either side of the body.

8 Glue the tail to the back end of the mouse.

9 Fold the nightcap, and glue the long sides together. Place the cap on the mouse, and glue it in place. Fold the cap to the front. Glue the yellow pompom on the end of the cap.

10 Glue two stars together, and glue them to the mouse's front paws.

11 Cut the top point off the star cover, even with the other two points to make a straight line. Glue this point as a back straight up and down where it was cut off.

12 Paint the star box inside and out with two coats of Luscious Lemon. Stencil STAR on the front with Cool Blue. Paint the wood star with two coats of Luscious Lemon acrylic. Varnish all pieces with two coats.

13 Glue rickrack around the edges of the star. Glue the wood star above the "R."

14 Glue the star box to the top of the cover. Glue the mouse on top.

More Thoughts

PAINT A SET OF BOXES TO KEEP BABY ITEMS IN. STACK THEM AND SET A MOUSE ON TOP.

Sail Away on a Sea of Stars

"Here Come the Animals" Peg Shelf

Babies come with such cute accessories. SWEET
TINY HATS AND COLORFUL SLEEPERS HUNG FROM THE PEGS WILL
MAKE THE SHELF AN ADORABLE ADDITION TO THE NURSERY.

SIZE: 24" LONG

YOU WILL NEED:

- 8" x 22½" plush pieces: 1 White, 1 Heather Gray,
  1 Cashmere Tan
- 9" x 12" felt piece: Misty Blue
- 6 oz. polyester fiberfill
- 3 black 5mm eye beads
- ½" yellow pompom
- ¼" black pompom
- Nine 1" wood stars
- Two 2" wood stars
- 1½" wood star
- Matching threads
- 6" white chenille stem

- DecoArt Crafter's Acrylic: Luscious Lemon, Cool
  Blue, White
- DecoArt DuraClear satin varnish
- ½ yd. of Wrights rainbow rickrack
- 24" wood peg shelf
- Wood glue
- 2 small brackets

Tools: Scissors, glue gun and low temp. glue sticks,
needle, 1" foam brushes, palette or plastic lid, pins,
blush.

Nursery Décor

1 Cut the required pattern pieces from the pattern sheet. Cut all pieces from plush and felt, including a 2" x 2½" tail for the giraffe.

2 These animals can be glued or sewn. Instructions are given for gluing. These animals are assembled with plush, wrong sides together.

3 Run glue along the inside edge of the animal pieces, and press the pieces firmly together. Stuff the bodies lightly. Glue the opening shut.

4 For eyes, secure the thread at the back of the head. Take a needle through to the front of the head at the mark. Slide the bead on the needle. Return the needle to the back, and secure the thread. Repeat for all three animals.

5 Pleat the ears of the elephant and mouse at the marks, and glue them in place on the heads. Glue their tails in place.

6 For the mouse, glue the back seam of the nightcap. Glue it on the mouse's head. Glue the point to the front edge of the hat. Glue the yellow pompom at the tip.

7 Glue the black nose pompom in place. Blush the cheeks. Glue the arms and legs to the body, matching Xs. Cut a 6" piece of rickrack, and glue it around the mouse's neck.

8 Cut a thin strip of Misty Blue felt, and glue it to the chenille stem. Glue the chenille stem to the mouse's body front and his paw.

9 Glue a 6" piece of rickrack around the neck of the elephant.

10 For the giraffe, fringe the tail ½" along the longer side. Roll the tail into a tight cylinder. Glue the tail to the body. Glue the hooves, spots, ears, and horns in place. Glue 5" of rickrack around the neck of the giraffe.

11 Paint all the stars with a couple of coats of Luscious Lemon. Paint the shelf with three coats of White.

12 Press the end of the brush around the edge of the shelf, alternating Cool Blue and Luscious Lemon to make 1" wide blocks of color.

13 Paint the center of the shelf with two coats of Cool Blue. Add a few drops of White to lighten the blue slightly. Brush lightly across the center of the shelf, creating a misty look.

14 Glue the 1" wood stars in place on the front of the shelf. Apply two coats of varnish to the shelf and all the stars.

15 Alternating the animals and 2" stars, glue them to the top of the shelf. Glue the 1½" star to the end of the mouse's chenille stem wand.

16 Attach brackets to the back of the shelf and hang. The wall will keep the animals straight.

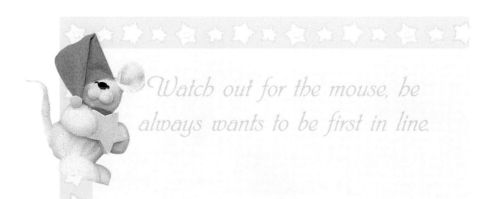

Watch out for the mouse, he always wants to be first in line.

Sail Away on a Sea of Stars

Elvis the Elephant

Always a favorite character, ELEPHANTS WITH THEIR BIG EARS, TRUNKS, AND ROUND BODIES ARE FUN TO CREATE. "ELVIS" IS AN EASY NO SEW PROJECT. A WHIMSICAL ADDITION TO ANY SHELF OR DRESSER, HE WILL KEEP A GENTLE EYE ON A SLEEPING WEE ONE.

SIZE: 12" HIGH

Nursery Décor

- 4" and 6" foam balls
- ½ yd. Heather Gray plush felt
- 1 oz. polyester fiberfill
- 2 black 8mm eye beads
- 1½" wood star
- DecoArt Crafter's Acrylic Luscious Lemon
- ½ yd. of 1" yellow polka dot grosgrain ribbon
- ½ yd. Needleloft white craft cord

Tools: Sharp scissors, glue gun and low temp. glue sticks, compass, foam brush, palette or plastic lid, invisible marker, pins, knife, blush, ruler.

1 Review Covering Foam Shapes on page 10. Cut the required pattern pieces from the pattern sheet. From Heather Gray plush felt, cut the pattern pieces and cut one 5", 10", and 16" circle and four 4" x 11" leg strips.

2 With a knife, cut a thin slice off one side of each foam ball. Cover the large ball with the 16" circle and the smaller ball with the 10" circle. Glue the 5" circle to cover the flat side of the ball. This will be the bottom of the body.

3 With the sharp point of a scissors, make holes for the eyes, ¾" apart at the front of the head. Glue the black eye beads in place. Blush the cheeks.

4 With wrong sides together, glue along the edges of the trunk, leaving the end open. Stuff slightly. Run glue around the inside edge of the end. Center and glue the trunk just below the eyes.

5 Pleat the ears on the lines. Glue an ear on either side of the head, in line with the eyes.

6 Glue the bottom of the head to the top end of the body.

7 With wrong sides together, glue the tail pieces together. Glue the tail to the back end of the body.

8 Fold 1½" in on the leg strips, making them 2½" wide, and glue. Roll the strip tightly, like a jelly roll. Glue the edges in place.

9 Place glue on the thinner ends of the legs. Glue the legs to the bottom of the body, along the edge of the 5" circle, with ½" to 1" between legs. Angle the front legs out slightly so the elephant will stand.

10 Glue the ribbon around the elephant's neck. Trim off the excess.

11 Paint the star with two coats of Luscious Lemon. Glue it to the end of the cord. Tie the other end around the trunk.

More Thoughts

MAKE A TWIN. TO CREATE A SOFT VERSION OF THIS FRIENDLY FELLOW, SEW ALL THE PIECES AND STUFF THE GATHERED CIRCLES WITH FIBERFILL; USE SAFETY EYES. "THE ELEPHANTS CAME IN TWO BY TWO."

Sail Away on a Sea of Stars

Sleepy Mouse

Tiny fuzzy creatures have such an appeal AS ACCENTS IN A NURSERY. THIS LITTLE SLEEPY MOUSE IS A PERFECT ADDITION TO THE STAR MOBILE OR ANY LITTLE SPACE THAT NEEDS A TOUCH OF CHARM.

SIZE: 5"

- 2" foam ball
- 2⁵⁄₁₆" x 3" foam egg
- Two 1¹⁵⁄₁₆" x 1½" foam eggs
- ⅛ yd. White plush felt
- 9" x 12" felt piece: Misty Blue
- ½" yellow pompom
- ¼" black pompom
- 1 yd. black embroidery floss
- 6" thin wire

Tools: Scissors, glue gun and low temp. glue sticks, embroidery needle, invisible marker, pins, blush.

1 Review Covering Foam Shapes on page 10. Cut the required pattern pieces from the pattern sheet. Cut the pieces from plush and felt.

2 Cut a thin slice off the foam ball (head) and 2⁵⁄₁₆" x 3" foam egg (body). Cut one smaller foam egg in half lengthwise for the back feet. Cut a third off each long side of the other small egg for front paws.

3 From White plush, cut a 5" circle to cover the head; ovals for the egg shapes 2" larger than the shape; and ovals the same size to cover the bottoms of the shapes.

4 Cover the tops and bottoms of all foam pieces.

5 With three strands of black embroidery floss, anchor the floss at the back of the head. Take a needle through the head to the front. Make a ¼" stitch, and take the needle back

through the head. Repeat for the other eye stitch and mouth stitch. Secure the floss at the back of the head.

6 Glue the black pompom nose at the top of the mouth stitch. Pleat the ears, and glue the bottom edges. Glue the ears to either side of the head, above the eyes. Blush the cheeks.

7 Glue the back of the head to the narrow end of the egg. Angle the back feet out, and glue them under the bottom end. Angle the front paws out, and glue them under the head.

8 Glue wire between the tail pieces, right sides out. Cut off the excess. Curl the tail. Glue the tail to the back end of the mouse.

9 Fold the nightcap and glue the long sides together. Glue the cap on the mouse's head. Fold the cap to the front. Glue it in place. Glue the yellow pompom on the end.

*'Twas a night before baby
and all through the house
not a creature was stirring
not even a sleepy mouse.*

Sail Away on a Sea of Stars

Starry Dreams Mobile

Mobiles are meant to be INTERESTING FOR BABIES, BUT OFTEN THE BEST VIEW ISN'T FROM THE CRIB. THIS MOBILE IS CHARMING FROM ANY ANGLE. THE HOOK AND LOOP FASTENER ATTACHES DIFFERENT FUNNY FACES TO THE BOTTOM OF THE LARGE STAR. CHANGE THEM OFTEN TO DELIGHT BABY WITH A NEW FRIEND.

SIZE: 36" TO 48" LONG

YOU WILL NEED:

- 1" x 9" foam star
- 1 yd. Light Yellow felt
- 9" x 12" felt pieces: 1 Blush Pink, 1 Misty Blue, 1 White, 1 Black
- 6 oz. polyester fiberfill
- 1 skein white embroidery floss
- 1 yd. pink embroidery floss
- Matching threads
- ½ yd. hook and loop fastener

Tools: Scissors, glue gun and low temp. glue sticks, sewing machine, embroidery needle, invisible marker, ruler.

1 Cut the required pattern pieces from the pattern sheet. Cut out the felt pieces.

2 Using the foam star as a template, cut out two Light Yellow felt stars. Cut a 1" x 36" strip of Light Yellow felt. Glue a felt star to the back and front of the foam. Glue the strip along the sides of the star. Trim off the excess.

3 Match up the felt stars in pairs. Topstitch close to the edge, leaving an opening. Stuff the stars. Finish top stitching the stars shut.

4 For the funny faces (in the diagrams), cut two White 3" circles for each face. Use three strands of pink embroidery floss to create the mouth stitches. Start at the nose, and make a stitch to the center dot and then to either side. Glue the ear pieces together, and then glue them just under the edge of the face circle. Glue two circles together, and cut two 2" pieces of hook and loop to glue to the back of the circle. Glue the other end of the hook and loop to the bottom of the star. For the B face, outline stitch the mouth. Glue the eyes and nose in place. Finish the same as A.

5 Anchor six strands of white embroidery floss with a large knot in the top end of each star point. Take the needle down through the foam star. Place two of the larger stars at opposite points, and sew floss to the top point of the stars, hanging them at 7" and 10" lengths.

6 Hang the smaller stars on the remaining points at 6", 7", and 12" lengths.

7 See pages 70–71 to make the Sleepy Mouse.

8 Anchor the floss at the center of the foam star. Take the needle through the center of the Sleepy Mouse to the bottom of the large star, approximately 11". Anchor the thread at the top of the large star, and take it to the smaller star, approximately 9" (not shown in photo). Attach the remainder of the floss to the top of the small star.

9 Hang the mobile at the required height.

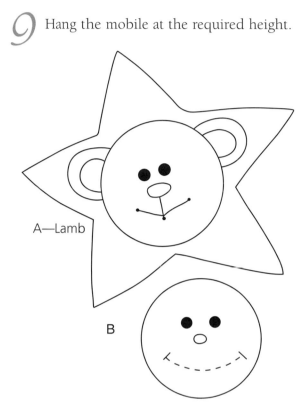

A—Lamb

B

More Thoughts

MAKE INDIVIDUAL STARS TO HANG IN THE WINDOW OR ON THE DOOR.

As the stars circle the sky gently and the sleepy mouse sways over a quiet crib, enjoy the perfection of the moment and hold it close to your heart.

Sail Away on a Sea of Stars

Sail Away Wall Hanging

My daughter, Amanda, was such a happy baby. SHE WOULD WAKE UP FROM A NAP AND COO AWAY AS SHE WATCHED HER FAVORITE PICTURE ON THE WALL. THIS WALL HANGING IS A WHIMSICAL PIECE TO DELIGHT YOUR LITTLE ONE, GUARANTEED TO PRODUCE MANY SMILES. IT'S QUICKLY PUT TOGETHER WITH FUSIBLE WEBBING AND A SIMPLE OUTLINE STITCH.

SIZE: 20" x 30"

Nursery Décor

- 1¼ yd. Light Yellow felt
- ⅓ yd. Misty Blue felt
- 6" felt squares: Baby Pink, Walnut Brown, White
- ⅙ yd. of Cashmere Tan and Heather Gray plush felt
- ½ yd. yellow and white cotton star fabric
- 6 oz. polyester fiberfill
- 6 black 6mm eye beads
- ½" white pompom

- Embroidery floss skeins: 1 pink, 1 black, 1 blue
- 20" of ¼" dowel
- 1 yd. fusible web
- 1 package PeelnStick
- Fabri-Tac glue

Tools: Wave-edge and scallop-edge scissors, scissors, embroidery needle, sewing needle, iron and ironing board, ruler, blush.

1 Refer to the photo and diagram (next page) while following the directions.

2 Cut the required pattern pieces from the pattern sheet. Cut the appropriate pieces from felt and plush.

3 **For the wall hanging**

a. Cut one 20" x 30" and one 2" x 20" piece of Light Yellow felt, and cut one 17" x 27" piece from the star print fabric. Using scallop-edge scissors, cut two strips 1" x 28" and two strips 1" x 18" from Misty Blue felt.

b. Sew the 2" x 20" yellow strip along the back of the 20" x 30" piece for the dowel, 1" down from the top. Sew it along both long sides of the strip.

c. Following the manufacturer's directions, center and fuse the star print over top of the Light Yellow felt. Overlap the Misty Blue strips along the edge of the star print, and fuse in place. Trim off any excess along either edge.

4 **For the ark**

a. Using an 8" circle as a pattern, measure and cut across 1" above the center of the circle. Cut out two circles from the Misty Blue felt.

b. For the back of the ark, cut a 7" square from Misty Blue felt. Fold the edges together. Starting 3" down the fold, trim the outside edges of one end to a rounded center point.

c. With scallop-edge scissors and Light Yellow felt, cut one strip ½" x 8" and another ½" x 14". Cut out the White felt heart. Use PeelnStick to apply the heart to the center front of the ark.

d. Align the two bottom pieces of the ark. Topstitch around all sides. Using PeelnStick, affix the ark back to the wall hanging. Glue trim along the back edge and across the front of the ark. Glue the edges of the curved sides of the ark front, starting at the 1" mark of the ark back.

5 **For the elephant**

a. Cut two 6" circles for the head and body, and cut two 2" x 4" leg strips from Heather Gray plush felt. Baste along the edge of the circles. Pull the stitches, stuff, and pull the stitches tight, creating two soft stuffed ball shapes. Secure the threads. (The gathered area is the back of the ball.)

b. Anchor the thread at the back of one stuffed ball, go through to the front ½" from the center, and slide on the black eye bead. Take the needle to the back and through to the front again. Repeat for the second eye. Secure the thread at the back of the head.

c. Topstitch along the edges of the trunk, leaving one end open. Stuff slightly. Center and glue the trunk to the front of the head, two thirds of the way down.

d. Pleat the ears on the indicated lines. Run glue along the edge. Glue the ears to the head, in line with the eyes.

e. Blush ears and cheeks.

Sail Away on a Sea of Stars

f. Overlap the short edges of the leg strips by ¼", and stitch them into cylinders. Glue a Baby Pink hoof into the end of each leg. Stuff slightly.

g. Pat the other ball into an oval for the body. Sew or glue the head to the top of the body. Run glue around the other inner edge end of the leg. With your fingers, tightly pinch in the end. Repeat for the other leg.

h. With the seam down, glue the pinched end of the legs to the bottom of the head where it joins the body.

6 For the giraffe

a. Cut a 6" circle, 2" x 6" strip (neck), and two 2½" x 3" strips (legs) from Cashmere Tan plush felt. Cut two ⅝" x 2½" strips (hooves) from Walnut felt. Along the edge of the circle, baste, pull stitches, stuff, pull stitches tight, and secure threads. Pat the ball into an oval shape.

b. Repeat steps for eyes as for the elephant (#5 b.), placing the eyes two thirds of the way up the face. Glue the ears and horns to the top of the head. Glue the nose pieces to the front of face. Glue two spots to the head.

c. Overlap the Walnut hoof strip by ¼" along the 2½" edge of the leg strip. Repeat for the sec-

ond leg. Overlap the short sides of the leg and neck strips by ¼", and stitch them into cylinders. Stuff slightly.

d. Glue two spots to the neck and one spot to the front of each leg. With the seam at the back, run glue along the inside edge of the neck. Glue the neck to the bottom of the head. Repeat for the legs. Glue the legs to either side of the neck, 1" apart.

7 With two strands of blue floss, outline stitch around all edges of the stars. On the largest star, a middle star, and a small star outline stitch a pink smile. With black floss, stitch ½" sleeping eyes on the middle and small star. Sew eye beads to the large star. Glue the edges of the nightcap together. Glue the pompom at the end. Slip the cap over the top of the large star. Fold the hat over, and glue the point to the star edge.

8 With 2" squares of PeelnStick, affix the stars in place on the wall hanging.

9 Stuff the bottom of the ark slightly. Insert the animals into the ark. Glue or stitch them in place.

10 Slide the dowel through the back, hang, and admire.

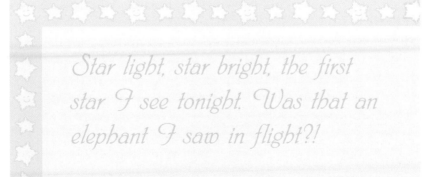

Star light, star bright, the first star I see tonight. Was that an elephant I saw in flight?!

1"　1"

3"

14"

2¼"

3¼"

11¾"

3"

2"

2⅛"

3¼"

SAIL AWAY WALL HANGING

Animal Ark

Lightweight foam shapes and cheery felt BRING THIS PROJECT TO LIFE. A PERFECT NURSERY DÉCOR ADDITION TO A SHELF OR CHEST OF DRAWERS, THIS ARK IS GUARANTEED TO PRODUCE BABY SMILES.

SIZE: 9" HIGH

YOU WILL NEED:

- 7⅜" x 1³⁄₁₆" round foam disc
- 3" and 5" flat foam hearts
- 2" foam ball
- 2½" x 1⅞" foam egg
- 9" x 12" felt pieces: 3 Misty Blue, 1 Light Yellow, 1 Baby Pink, 1 Walnut, 1 White
- 6" x 22" plush felt pieces: 1 Heather Gray, 1 Cashmere Tan

- 4 black 5mm beads
- 1½" wood star
- DecoArt Crafter's Acrylic: Luscious Lemon

Tools: Scallop-edge scissors, sharp scissors, glue gun and low temp. glue sticks, pins, knife, blush, ruler, invisible marker, small foam brush.

1 Review Covering Foam Shapes (page 10). Cut the required pattern pieces from the pattern sheet. Cut out the felt pieces.

2 Cut the foam disc in half. Cut a slice from the foam ball and the long side of the foam egg.

3 Using one half of the disc as a template, cut a front and back for the ark from Misty Blue felt. Glue the disc halves together. Glue the felt front and back to the disc.

4 Cut the top and side strips for the ark from Light Yellow felt, 2½" x 8" and 2½" x 12". Glue them in place along the edges.

5 Using the 5" foam heart as a template, cut one heart from Misty Blue felt, 1" larger all the way around, for the front. Cut one 5" Misty Blue heart for the back. Glue the front to the heart, covering the sides. Glue the back in place.

6 Using Light Yellow felt and the 3" foam heart template, cut a front 1" larger all the way around. From White felt, use scallop-edge scissors to cut a heart the same size as the front. Glue the Light Yellow felt to the front and sides of the foam heart. Glue White felt to the front, over the Light Yellow.

7 From Light Yellow felt, cut a decorative band for the top edge of the ark, two strips ¾" x 12". Trim one edge with scallop-edge scissors. Glue the band around the top edge of the ark.

8 Cut a decorative band from the Light Yellow felt for the edge of the 5" heart, 1¼" x 12". Trim both edges with scallop-edge scissors.

9 Fold the band in half. Glue from the bottom point of the heart up either side. (The top 3" of the heart won't be covered.)

10 Turn the heart upside down, and place it 1½" down at the center back of the disc. Glue it in place.

11 Glue the small heart to the center of the ark front. Paint and glue the wood star to the front.

12 **For the elephant**

a. From the Heather Gray plush felt, cut a 4" circle for the head front, 1½" circle for the head back, and two 2" x 4" strips for the legs.

b. Cover the front and back of the head, and glue the plush in place. With the wrong sides together, glue along the edges of the trunk, leaving the bottom end open.

c. Cut a thin strip of scrap plush to slide in the trunk. Place a thin line of glue along the inside end of the trunk. Center and glue the truck on the head, about two thirds of the way down the face. Just above the trunk, make holes for the eyes, 1" apart. Glue black beads in place.

d. Pleat the ears on the indicated lines. Run glue along the edge. Glue the ears to the head in line with the eyes.

e. Blush the ears and cheeks.

f. Overlap the short edges of the leg strips by ¼", and glue them into cylinders. Glue the pink hoofs into the end of each leg.

g. Run glue around the other inner edge end of the leg. With your fingers, pinch the end in. Repeat for the other leg.

h. With the seam down, glue the pinched end of each leg to the bottom of the head.

13 **For the giraffe**

a. From the Cashmere Tan plush felt, cut a 2" x 6" strip for the neck and two 2½" x 3" strips for the legs. From the Walnut felt, cut two ⅝" x 2½" strips for the hooves.

b. Measure up ¾" from the narrow end of the egg. Press in with your fingers to indent by ¾", creating the front of the face.

c. Lay the flat side of the egg down on the wrong side of the Cashmere Tan plush felt. For the front of the head, cut a piece of plush 2" larger all the way around. Cut a piece of plush for the bottom of the head the same size as the flat side of the egg. Cover the head front and bottom.

d. At the indent in the head, make holes ½" apart for the eyes. Glue the eyes in place. Glue the ears and horns to the top of the head. Glue the nose pieces to the front of the face. Glue three spots to the head.

e. Overlap the Walnut hoof strip by ¼", along the 2½" edge of the leg strip. Repeat for the sec-

ond leg. Overlap the short sides of the leg and neck strips by ¼", and glue them into cylinders.

f. Glue two spots to the neck and one to the front of each leg. With the seam at the back, run glue along the inside edge of the neck. Glue the neck to the bottom of the head. Repeat for the legs. Glue the legs to either side of the neck, 1" apart.

14 Glue the elephant head and the giraffe neck bottoms to the top of the ark, 1" apart.

Imagine adventures for these fuzzy friends, and tell the stories to your baby.

Nursery Décor

Notes

Make a wish

Nursery Décor

Chapter 5

B Is for Baby

A simple sophisticated look is featured in this room. The classic alphabet adorns the room. The black "Scotty" dog adds a touch of whimsy as well as punch to this serene room. Projects show how purchased items can be given a handcrafted look, from curtains to blankets. Come inside and be creative with easy style.

Memory Box

The first year of a baby's life IS FILLED WITH MANY MEMORABLE MOMENTS. ALL OF WHICH PARENTS WISH TO CAPTURE IN A VARIETY OF WAYS, ESPECIALLY PHOTOS. SPECIAL BABY GIFTS, CARDS, OR THAT CHERISHED FIRST OUTFIT ALL NEED A PLACE TO BE STORED LOVINGLY. A SIMPLE CARDBOARD BOX WITH COVER CAN BE TRANSFORMED INTO A WONDERFUL MEMORY BOX TO HOLD THOSE PRECIOUS MEMORIES. A COORDINATING SET OF BOXES WOULD BE ATTRACTIVE IF MORE THAN ONE BOX IS NEEDED. (I FILLED ONE BOX FOR THE FIRST MONTH!)

THERE ARE MANY ACID FREE STORAGE BOXES AND TISSUES AVAILABLE AT CRAFT AND PHOTOGRAPHY STORES. A LARGER STANDARD BOX CAN BE FILLED WITH SMALLER ACID-FREE BOXES TO CATEGORIZE AND PROTECT THE BABY ITEMS.

FINISHED BOX SIZE: 12" X 20" X 8"

YOU WILL NEED:

- A rectangular box with cover (12" x 20" x 8", cover has 1½" sides)
- 3 pieces of 11½" x 19½" box weight cardboard
- 2½ yd. cotton or polycotton fabric (a small all-over print is best)
- 9" x 12" felt pieces: 1 Walnut Brown, 1 Black

- 1 yd. polyester quilt batting
- 2 yd. each of ⅜" and ⅝" grosgrain ribbon

Tools: Scissors, glue gun and low temp. glue sticks, rotary cutter and mat, iron, pressing board.

1 (Directions are given for this specific box as well as for a box of any size.) Measure the box dimensions. Cut a strip of quilt batting to go around the box sides. The piece should start 2" from the top of the box (cover will fit better). This box required a strip 6" x 64", which was pieced. Cut a piece to cover the top and sides. Run a thin line of glue along the edges of the box and cover. Gently pat the quilt batting in place.

2 To cover the outside of the box, cut one strip of polycotton fabric 4" wider and 2" longer than the box. This box required a strip 12" x 66". Wrap the box with the fabric, leaving 2" extra at the top and bottom.

3 Turn one edge under, and overlap the fabric at the back of the box. Pull the fabric smooth but not too tight. Glue this edge in place.

4 Fold the fabric at the top of the box to the inside of the box. Neatly overlap the fabric corners, just like wrapping a present. Glue along the edges on the inside.

5 Fold the fabric under the bottom of the box, neatly overlapping the corners. Trim some of the extra fabric, if desired.

6 For the cover, cut a piece of polycotton fabric 4" larger all the way around, including the sides. This box required a piece 20" x 28". Wrap the cover in the same way as the bottom of the box.

7 Measure in 3" from the sides of the covered box cover, and glue the ⅜" grosgrain ribbon. Glue the ribbon at the inside edge of the cover. Glue the ⅜" grosgrain ribbon ¼" to the outside of the wider ribbon. Repeat for the front of the box, gluing the ribbon under the bottom 2" and the inside top 2".

8 For the inside sides of the box, cut a polycotton fabric strip 1" wider and longer than the inside measurement of the box. This box required a strip 9" x 65". Press the fabric under ½" along the shorter side and both long sides of the strip.

9 As shown in the diagrams, the inside of the cover and box and the bottom of the box are neatly covered. Measure the inside of the cover and both the inside and outside of the box bottom. These pieces will be about the same size. Add 1" to the measurements for the fabric pieces. This box required three pieces 13" x 21".

10 Press under ½" along each side of each piece. Place the cardboard pieces (11½" x 19½" for this box) centered on the wrong side of each of these pieces. Run a line of glue around the edges, and glue the fabric in place. Overlap the corners as if you were wrapping a package. Run glue along the edges of the inside cover of the box, box bottom, and inside box bottom.

11 Using the pattern sheet, cut a letter "B" from Walnut felt. Glue the "B" to the black felt, and cut around the outside edge, leaving a ¼" border. Glue it to the center front of the box.

Inside Memory Box

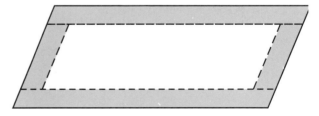

Wrong Side of Memory Box Bottom

More Thoughts

MAKE THE BOX AS A SPECIAL BABY SHOWER GIFT. FILL IT WITH BABY ITEMS SUCH AS A BABY BOOK, CALENDAR, STICKERS, AND, OF COURSE, LOTS OF LOVE.

Alphabet Blanket

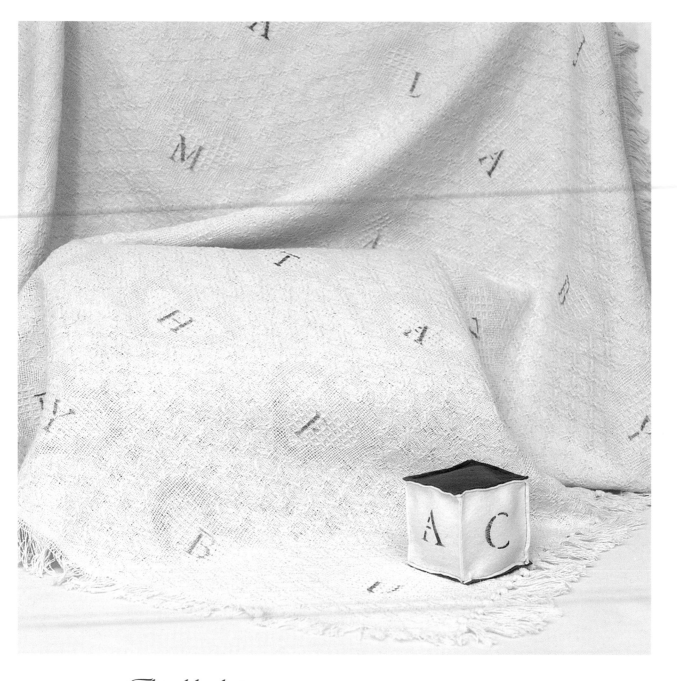

This blanket IS ANOTHER PROJECT FOR BOTH BABY AND PARENTS. I
REMEMBER SO MANY NIGHTS OF ROCKING IN THE EARLY DAYS. IT'S
COMFORTING TO HAVE A COZY COVER TO CUDDLE IN DURING THOSE TIMES.

SIZE: 96" x 120"

Nursery Décor

- 96" x 120" cream cotton blanket (A common design is one with hearts, as used here. The stencil letters fit perfectly in the heart centers.)
- 1½" Plaid Monogram Forum Classic stencil
- ⅜" stencil brush
- Folkart Acrylic Burnt Umber Paint

Tools: Paper towel, iron, pressing cloth and board, scrap of fabric, plastic lid container, tape, pins.

1 Wash the blanket according to the instructions on the care label. Place a piece of cardboard under the blanket. Pin the blanket to the pressing board. Review Stenciling on page 19.

2 I found cutting the letters apart made stenciling easier. Cut around them very carefully, leaving as much stencil as possible around each letter.

3 Practice stenciling on a scrap piece of fabric. Place a small amount of paint on a plastic lid. Dip the end of the brush into the paint. Hold the brush straight up and down. With a circular motion, brush onto the paper towel until the color is a soft brown.

4 Arrange the letters in a random order pleasing to you. Select a letter. Place it in the center of the heart. While holding the letter stencil down, firmly tape it to the blanket. Move the brush in a circular motion, working from the top of the letter to the bottom. Go slowly, filling in the textured area. (More than one letter may be done with the brush before adding more paint.)

5 Having letters vary in shading gives a more handcrafted look to the blanket.

6 Continue stenciling. When finished, heat set the letters with the iron.

Pull up a comfy rocker, cuddle a sleepy baby, and wrap up in this cozy blanket. Tender moments are made to remember.

B Is for Baby

$\mathcal{A}$BC Blocks

Babies love to grasp objects. THESE SOFT FELT
ALPHABET BLOCKS ARE DECORATIVE AS WELL AS EASY FOR BABY TO
HOLD AND, OF COURSE, TO THROW.

SIZE: 4" x 4"

Nursery Décor

YOU WILL NEED:

- 9" x 12" felt pieces: 2 Antique White, 1 Cinnamon, 1 Walnut
- 1½" Plaid Monogram Forum Classic stencil
- Folkart Acrylic Burnt Umber paint
- ⅜" stencil brush
- 6 oz. polyester fiberfill
- 1 yd. fusible interfacing
- 4" square template
- Matching threads

Tools: Scissors, sewing machine, needle, chalk pencil, iron and ironing board, plastic lid, pins, paper towel.

1 Use a 4" template to cut 10 Antique White, four Cinnamon, and four Walnut felt pieces.

2 Review Stenciling on page 19. Stencil a letter in the center of each Antique White block. "A," "B," "C," and "D" were used on the blocks here, but any of the letters can be placed on the blocks.

3 Follow the manufacturer's directions to fuse the interfacing to the back of each piece.

4 Assemble the blocks according to the diagram. Pin the squares together, and sew using a ⅛" topstitch. Leave a small opening in the center of one side to stuff. Sew the four sides together, and then sew the top and bottom in place.

5 Trim the threads, stuff the blocks, and sew the openings shut.

		1. C	
		2. C	
		3. WB	
1. AW	AW	AW	AW
2. AW	WB	AW	C
3. AW	AW	AW	AW
		1. C	
		2. WB	
		3. WB	

ABC Blocks Layout

Stack them and throw them without a care. Laugh with your baby as the blocks fly through the air.

B Is for Baby

"Shhh" Wall Hanging

BABY
SLEEP
DREAM
PEACE
QUIET
SHHH

This simple wall hanging IS GREAT FOR A BABY'S DOOR.
WHEN THE DOOR IS CLOSED, EVERYONE KNOWS IT'S QUIET TIME.

SIZE: 14" X 25"

Nursery Décor

- ⅓ yd. Antique White felt
- ⅓ yd. cotton print fabric
- 1½" Plaid Monogram Forum Classic stencil
- Folkart Acrylic Burnt Umber paint
- ⅜" stencil brush
- Two 14" pieces of ¼" dowel
- Matching threads

Tools: Scissors, sewing machine, needle, invisible ink pen, iron and ironing board, plastic lid, paper towel, scrap fabric, pins, ruler.

1 From the Antique White felt, cut one 10½" x 21½" piece. From the cotton print fabric, cut two 5" x 21½" strips and two 5" x 16½" strips.

2 Review Stenciling on page 19. Practice the words on scrap fabric.

3 Use invisible ink to draw guide lines on the felt, beginning 3" down from top and 1¼" from right. Stencil the words on these lines. Heat set with the iron.

4 Press the fabric strips in half, right sides out. With right sides together, pin the strips to the long sides of the wall hanging. Sew with ¼" seam.

5 Press in the short ends of the remaining two strips ½". Pin the right sides together to the bottom and top of the wall hanging. Sew. Press flat.

6 Insert a dowel piece into the top and bottom.

More Thoughts

STENCIL AND FRAME THE WORDS FOR THE WALL. STENCIL WORDS HERE AND THERE AROUND THE ROOM.

B Is for Baby

D is for Dog

Actually "S" is for "Scotty" WOULD HAVE BEEN APPROPRIATE, BUT MOST BABIES BEGIN WITH THE SOUND "D" UNLESS YOU HAVE A GENIUS. (OF COURSE, WE ALL DO, ESPECIALLY WITH THE FIRST.) THIS SIMPLE PILLOW USES PURCHASED PRE-CUT FELT PIECES. IT'S QUICK AND EASY.

SIZE: 9" x 18"

YOU WILL NEED:

- 9" x 12" felt pieces: 1 Antique White, 2 Cinnamon, 2 Walnut
- 6" x 14" black plush felt
- 16 oz. polyester fiberfill stuffing
- 6" of ⅝" grosgrain ribbon
- Matching threads

Tools: Scissors, sewing machine, needle, pins, ruler.

Nursery Décor

1 Cut the dog pattern piece from the pattern page. Cut two dogs from the black plush felt. Cut the grosgrain ribbon in half, and place one piece around the neck of each dog. Stitch in place on the wrong side edges of the neck.

2 Pin the dogs to the front of the Antique White felt. Center the dogs with their noses ¼" apart. Machine or hand stitch them in place.

3 With right sides together, pin the 12" sides of one Cinnamon felt piece to a Walnut felt piece. Sew a ¼" seam, and press. Repeat for the other two pieces, alternating colors. Leave a 4" opening in the center to turn the pillow.

4 Pin the Antique White piece to the center front. Topstitch along the edge.

5 Pin the pillow back to the front, right sides together. Refer to the Simple Pillow Style on page 18. Sew around the pillow, and turn.

6 Stuff the pillow. Sew the back opening shut.

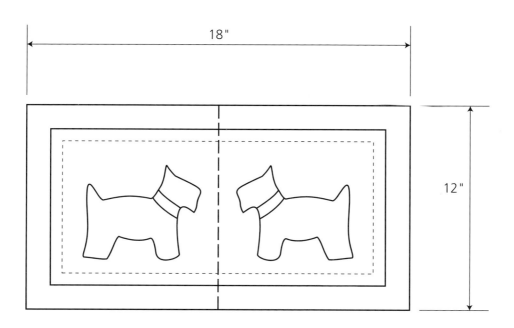

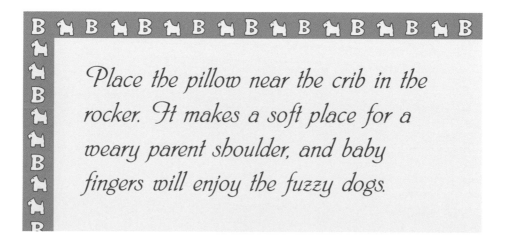

Place the pillow near the crib in the rocker. It makes a soft place for a weary parent shoulder, and baby fingers will enjoy the fuzzy dogs.

ABC Tissue Cover

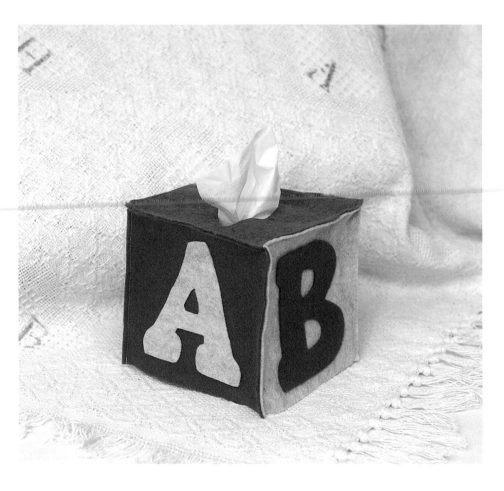

An indispensable product IS DRESSED UP WITH A SIMPLE COVER. THIS PROJECT CAN BE ADAPTED TO FIT ANY SIZE TISSUE BOX. IT CAN BE SEWN OR GLUED EASILY.

SIZE: 5" X 5½"

- 9" x 12" felt pieces: 2 Sandstone, 2 Cinnamon, 2 Walnut Brown
- ⅛ yd. fusible interfacing
- 6" x 12" of fusible web
- 5" x 5½" box of tissue
- 6" square template
- Matching threads

Tools: Scissors, sewing machine or glue gun and low temp. glue sticks, iron and ironing board, pins, chalk pencil.

1 Cut the letter pattern pieces from the pattern sheet. On the Sandstone felt, trace and cut out the letters "A" and "C." Cut "B" from Walnut Brown.

2 Using the 6" square template, cut out two squares of Walnut Brown and Sandstone felt and one square of Cinnamon felt.

3 Use the top of the tissue box as a pattern, and cut out the opening in the center of the Cinnamon square.

4 Following the manufacturer's instructions, apply fusible interfacing to the back of each square. Trim out the center of the Cinnamon square.

5 Apply fusible web to the back of the letters. Fuse "A" and "C" to the center of the Walnut Brown squares, and fuse "B" to the center of the Sandstone square.

6 Place the squares in order: "A," "B," "C," "blank." Glue or topstitch them together, ⅛" from the edges, to form a square. Pin the Cinnamon piece to the top, and glue or sew it in place.

7 Place the cover over the tissue box, and pull a tissue through the opening.

More Thoughts

MORE THAN ONE OF THESE IS DEFINITELY NEEDED. MAKE MORE TO MATCH OTHER ROOMS.

B Is for Baby

Babies spend time on the floor. THIS SOFT PLUSH MAT IS PERFECT TO SIT OR ROLL ON WITH SOME FAVORITE TOYS AND MOM OR DAD. A BAND OF COORDINATING TRIM GIVES THE RUG A SOPHISTICATED LOOK.

SIZE: 22" x 36"

Nursery Décor

- 1⅓ yd. Antique White plush felt
- 9" x 12" felt pieces: 2 Walnut Brown
- ⅛ yd. cotton print
- Matching threads

Tools: Scissors, sewing machine, iron and ironing board, needle, pins.

1 Cut the letter pattern pieces from the pattern sheet. Trace and cut the letters from Walnut Brown felt.

2 For the front and back of the rug, cut two 23" x 37" pieces from the Antique White plush.

3 With right sides together, pin the front to the back. With a ¼" seam, sew completely around, leaving a 6" opening on one side to turn the rug.

4 Trim the corners. Turn the rug right side out. Sew the opening shut.

5 Pin the letter "B" in the center of the rug. Spacing "A" and "C" 1" apart from "B" on either side, pin in place. Topstitch in place.

6 From the cotton print, cut two 1½" x 35" and two 1½" x 22" strips. Press all sides under ¼". Measure in 1" from the edge of the rug front, and pin the strips along this line.

7 Overlap the strips at the corners, trimming off any excess. Turn one end under ¼" at each corner. Topstitch in ⅛" along all sides.

8 If you're using the rug on a wood, tile, or vinyl floor, attach an anti-slip product underneath.

Remember the ABCs of life–
Always Be Creative.

B Is for Baby

Scotty

The simplest of shapes can give babies great pleasure. My daughter, Katy, fell in love with "bunny," a receiving blanket with a ball of fiberfill tied in one corner and two strips for ears. Painted whiskers and nose completed "bunny." Ten years later, he is still a cherished friend.

Size: 8"

YOU WILL NEED:

- ⅓ yd. black plush felt
- 8 oz. polyester fiberfill
- 1 yd. ⅝" grosgrain ribbon
- Matching threads

Tools: Scissors, sewing machine, needle.

1 Cut the required pattern pieces from the pattern sheet. Trace and cut the pieces from plush felt.

2 With right sides together, sew the pieces, leaving an opening where indicated. Clip the curves.

3 Turn the right side out. Stuff the feet firmly and the tummy a little softer.

4 Sew the opening shut.

5 Use grosgrain ribbon to tie a bow around the neck, stitching it firmly in place so it won't come off.

This little "Scotty" can be taught to do many tricks.

Notes

Always be creative

Chapter 6
Windows and Walls Simple Magic

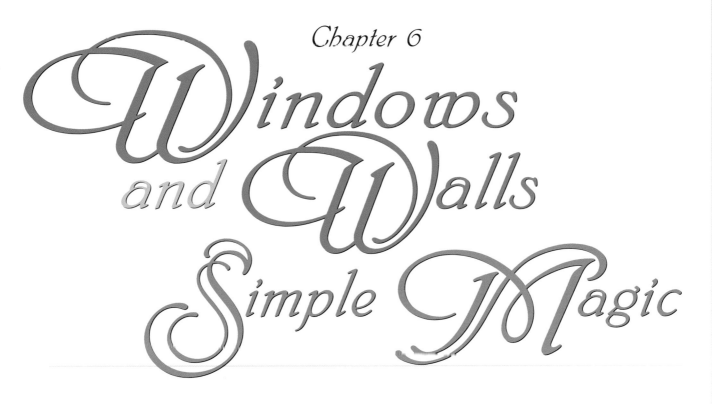

Once upon a time, there were plain walls and windows.

Sometimes putting a whole room together can be an intimidating venture. What to do with walls or windows is always a big question. But great looks can be put together easily by anyone. There are many wonderful products that make wall treatments simple. For non-sewers, window treatments can be created by customizing purchased panels or sheets. Fusible products allow fabric to be transformed into attractive window treatments.

Where to start is often the hardest decision. I often begin with a piece I just love. For example, the "Sail Away on a Sea of Stars" nursery began with the Animal Ark project. I took the project to match paint for the walls. It could be a special picture or cherished ornament. I believe in beginning with anything that inspires you, something that you love to look at. Create a room around it, and it should be a successful endeavor.

This chapter will look at each room and explain how easy it is to create the treatments used. Pattern pieces from some of the projects in the book are turned into wall stencils or appliqués for curtains.

Remember this is a room for you and your baby. You will spend time with your baby every day in this room. If your choices make you feel happy and comfortable, then your baby will feel the same. Babies are a wonder and a joy to create space for. Whatever you do they will love, so relax, jump in, and let your imagination take flight.

Tips, Tools, and Practical Things to Know

WALLS

When decorating a nursery or child's room, it's important to remember to use safe, easy-to-clean products. Many companies have lines of wallpaper and paints designed especially for babies' and children's rooms. They often come with a lifetime guarantee. The BEHR® Kids' Color Collection has such a guarantee and wonderful colors with names like Baby Lotion, Sweet Smile, and Bootie Time. Home improvement centers usually have an informed staff that can help. Paint companies have colorful handouts with examples of techniques in a variety of rooms. Pick good quality paints, rollers, and brushes. Sea sponges, rags, and cheesecloth are used along with a faux glaze to create several wall finishes.

Thousands of stencil designs are available for every theme imaginable. The designs can coordinate walls, fabrics, and furniture. Stencil brushes are produced for both hard and soft surfaces. When working with any paint technique, it's helpful to start with a sample board. Craft acrylic paints come in hundreds of colors and small two ounce bottles. Use poster board to experiment with ideas before you try them on a wall. If you don't like the results, just try another board until you're satisfied.

If painting isn't your style, wallpaper and coordinating borders can create enchanting rooms. There are delightful collections in every theme possible. Special children's collections are lively and durable. A wallpaper trough, knife, and brush are all tools that will be available where you purchase your paper. Take accurate measurements of the room before going shopping. A rough drawing would also be a good idea. When picking out papers, check that they all have the same lot numbers. This way the color will be exact. When applying wallpaper, be sure to follow the manufacturer's directions carefully. The International Wallcoverings Company has sweet borders and papers for nurseries.

Combining paint and paper or borders is another option. In Chapter 3 (Boys, Bears, and Baseball), a charming border gave some punch to a simple paint technique. Make sure the paint has completely dried for a couple of days before applying a border.

Tools: With all these projects there are several tools to have handy—paint trays, plastic containers, wallpaper trough, drop cloths, cleaning cloths, measuring tapes and sticks, pencils, chalk line, utility knives and scissors, and painter's tape. Also make sure the walls are smooth and clean before you begin. Grab an old shirt, put on some good music, and, baby, let's rock and roll

WINDOWS

As with all considerations in decorating a baby's room, safety is first. Any window treatments should not have dangling cords, ribbons, or strings of any kind. Full-length drapes are lovely but make sure they're anchored securely, perhaps shortening them when a little crawler is on the move. Keeping the cradle or crib a safe distance away from any window is a good idea.

Charming window treatments can be easily achieved these days whether you like to sew or not. The pattern companies have many wonderful designs to choose from. Fabric, quilt, and craft shops carry great fabrics and accessories for making any treatment imaginable. No-sew products, which just iron on, like the many innovative adhesives from Therm O Web, make it possible to use cute fabrics and produce a custom look. Felt panels will make a colorful window covering. Bright pieces like animals or flowers can be cut and glued to the panels. Matching multicolored tabs can be glued at the top and strung on a bright rod. When time is limited, purchased panels, curtains, or sheets can be accessorized with trims to produce a custom look.

Window treatments range from tailored to softly gathered panels. When you measure a window, allow for the tailored panels to be a few inches wider than the measurement across. Measure two to three times as wide for gathered panels. Determine the required length. If sewing, add several inches at the top for the rod casing and three to four inches at the bottom for the hem. There's a wide range of attractive rods available, or create your own with a brightly painted dowel, hooks for the wall, and a couple of cute toys to use as whimsical ends for the rod.

Other possibilities for windows include shutters and blinds. Perhaps you can create a custom blind with stenciling or by applying coordinating fabrics. Another option is to put pockets in a valance and stick toys in them. Hang a flower box or a shelf at the window ledge to display favorite pictures or toys. Visit home décor departments, and check out books and magazines for ideas. Remember always that this is your home and your baby, so pick colors and fabrics that make your heart smile. Create a special magical place for the both of you to enjoy every day.

The Enchanted Garden

In the Enchanted Garden nursery, the soft pink walls were achieved with a simple paint wash. It's a good technique to use if your walls have some slight imperfections to hide.

WALLS

YOU WILL NEED:

- 1 gallon white latex paint
- 1 quart BEHR Bella Rose latex paint
- BEHR Faux Glaze
- Cheesecloth

Tools: Refer to the beginning of the chapter, page 109.

1 First paint the walls with the white latex paint. Let dry thoroughly.

2 A soft pink, Bella Rose, latex paint was mixed with a glaze. Follow the manufacturer's directions for mixing the paint with the glaze, usually three parts glaze to one part paint. It takes very little paint. If you wish a stronger effect, experiment and add more paint. Let the walls dry thoroughly. Mix the glaze and paint in a small container.

3 Start any paint treatment behind a door or on another inconspicuous place in the room. This gives you a chance to get comfortable with the technique before hitting a main wall. If you're unhappy with the results in the beginning, just wipe it off. Keep a damp cloth handy at all times, and wipe mistakes off immediately, while the paint is still wet.

4 Dip a crumpled piece of cheesecloth into the glaze mixture, and gently rub it on the wall in a circular motion.

5 Keep turning the cloth as you dip it in the glaze. Replace the cloth when it's saturated. As you rub or "wash" (now you know where the name came from) the wall, the color will be a soft mixture of lighter and darker areas with the white coming through. It's a soft dreamy effect, perfect for an "enchanted" space.

More Thoughts

Use the bunny design from the garden lap quilt (page 24) as a border design. Cut bunnies from contact paper and place them jumping across the wall. Use the smaller version of the bunny from the Flowerpot Frame (page 32), and apply it to furniture.

The painted effect can also be applied to furniture. Use painter's tape to tape off parts of furniture. Apply the color, let dry, and remove the tape. Professional clean edges are achieved by this method, just be sure to use the correct tape and press it firmly in place. It's always amazing how paint can transform the worst looking piece of furniture into a precious addition to any room. Paint the legs a combination of white, pink, and mint green. Color wash the sides or the seats. Protect the furniture with a couple coats of clear acrylic varnish.

In the Enchanted Garden nursery, two twin striped sheets were used on the window. The wide hem was clipped open at either end to put the rod through. The bunny pattern from the Garden Lap Quilt was used to make the bunny valance, accented with the half carrots from the Ruffled Lamp. Wide sheer wired ribbon was tied into bows and attached to the edge of the panels.

This valance is on a small three-foot wide window. To create a larger valance, add more bunnies alternating with the carrots.

Nursery Décor

- ⅔ yd. white plush felt
- 6 oz. polyester fiberfill
- 2 carrots from the Ruffled Lamp (page 30)
- Bunny pattern from the Garden Lap Quilt (page 24)

- 3 yd. of 1½" sheer wired pastel ribbon
- Fabri-Tac glue
- White thread
- Scissors, pencil, needle

1 Cut out two bunnies from plush, reverse the pattern, and cut two more.

2 Align two bunny pieces together. Glue around the edges, leaving a small opening. Insert the fiberfill. Glue the openings shut. Use the pastel ribbon to tie a bow around the bunny's neck.

3 With needle and thread, attach the back of the bunnies and carrots to the top of the panels.

More Thoughts

HANG SOME CARROTS IN THE WINDOW. HAVE BUNNIES HOPPING ACROSS THE WINDOW LEDGE OR THE TOP OF THE CLOSET DOORS. CREATE A MOBILE.

Boys, Bears, and Baseball

When I saw this wallpaper border with the bears in sports outfits,
I knew it would be perfect for the room. The bears in their striped baseball uniforms were so cute and captured the color and theme of the room so well. The border is from the International Wallcoverings Company's wonderful "Bears and Company-Second Edition" collection. There's a wide range of borders and papers for children. The border in the room is placed at a height where baby can easily see it when in the crib or on the change table. When being rocked, baby will have a good view of all the bears.

Make up a story about the bears for your little one. Don't be surprised if your baby amuses himself by "talking" away to the furry fellows. A border along the baseboard is also a good idea for the older baby, putting it at his or her eye level when playing on a blanket or crawling.

The border is combined with a super-easy fun wall treatment. The walls were first painted white. Another paint was used in a tan shade over the top. A small bit of red paint and a fine brush create the stitch lines. Use the 4" baseball pattern from the Baseball Throw project for the balls on the wall. The balls are randomly spaced all over the wall to look like they were just thrown here and there.

Nursery Décor

WALLS

YOU WILL NEED:

- Latex paints: white, tan
- 2 oz. bottle red acrylic paint
- 4" ball from the Baseball Throw (page 48)
- White poster board
- Painter's tape

- Liner brush
- Scissors
- Pencil

Tools: See beginning of the chapter, page 109.

1 Paint the walls white. Let dry thoroughly.

2 Decide where the balls are to be placed on the walls.

3 Cut enough balls from poster board for one wall.

4 Form tape into loops, and fasten the balls to the wall securely.

5 Use the roller to carefully paint the wall with the tan, rolling gently over the poster board balls.

6 Gently remove the poster board, and the wall should be covered with balls.

7 Using the pattern as a guide, paint small stitch lines with the fine brush and red paint.

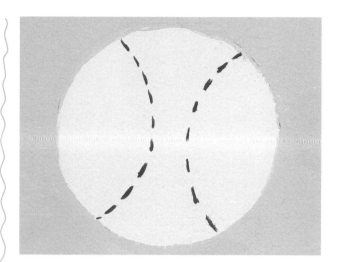

8 Alternate the angles of the stitch lines on the balls.

9 Repeat for the other walls. Let dry thoroughly.

10 Apply a border according to the manufacturer's directions.

More Thoughts

FOR THE WINDOW IN THIS "PLAY BALL!" ROOM, A SIMPLE BUT STRIKING TREATMENT WOULD BE VERY EFFECTIVE. A NAVY OR RED BLIND WITH STRIPES OR WOOD SHUTTERS WITH A SHELF OVER TOP OF THE WINDOW FOR SPORTS ACCESSORIES WOULD FINISH THE ROOM.

Sail Away on a Sea of Stars

This room is bright and cheerful. Even on the dullest of days, the room is lit with sunshine or starlight. Blue walls are accented with fluffy clouds and falling stars. This room is like entering a magical land high in the clouds. Again this is a very easy design to create. Clouds are sponged on, and stars from the Starry Dreams Mobile are used as stencils. The same pattern is used for the cute curtains on the window.

Nursery Décor

YOU WILL NEED:

- Latex paints: blue, white, yellow
- Star from Starry Dreams Mobile (page 78)
- 5" baseball from Bat and Ball (page 62)
- Poster board
- Painter's tape

- Sea sponge
- Pencil
- Scissors

Tools: See beginning of the chapter, page 109.

1 To create stencils, cut baseball and star patterns from the pattern sheet. Cut three 8" squares of poster board. Cut one piece of poster board 22" x 15".

2 Use half the 5" circle as a pattern to create the edges of a cloud. Referring to the photo, move the half circle around in an oval pattern to create a cloud. When satisfied with the shape, cut out the center of the cloud.

3 Draw the star patterns on the three squares of poster board. Cut them out to make the star stencils.

4 Paint the room blue. Let dry thoroughly.

5 Decide on the spacing of the clouds. In this nursery, the clouds are spaced about a foot apart.

6 Tape the cloud stencil to the wall. Dip the sea sponge in the white paint. Pat excess paint off on a rag or paper towel. Beginning at one end of the cloud, pat the sponge on the wall, covering the whole stencil area unevenly. Add more paint, if desired. Let dry. Repeat for each cloud.

7 When the clouds are finished and completely dry, stencil the stars on the clouds and walls.

8 Refer to the close up picture of the cloud. The stars are applied with the sponge in the same way that the cloud was. A couple of coats were applied to create a more solid color.

9 Have fun with the stars. Place them resting in the clouds or hanging two or three together.

The stencil cloud pattern used for the walls was also used to create a valance and appliqués for the curtains. The stars, made with the same pattern pieces used in the Starry Dreams Mobile, are gently stuffed and attached to the panels. The window shown is a three-foot by four-foot window. The curtain panels are each double the width of the window. At the bottom of each panel, a cloud was tacked on with stars from the mobile pattern.

YOU WILL NEED:

- 2 yd. white felt
- 2 yd. polyester quilt batt
- 8 oz. polyester fiberfill
- 5 stars from the Starry Dreams Mobile (page 78) two large, three small
- 5" baseball from Bat and Ball (page 62)
- 3 sheets of poster board

Tools: Scissors, sewing machine and matching thread, needle, pins, pencil, hooks.

1 Cut a piece of poster board the size of the valance required, plus an extra 2" for the seam. (If the window is large, make two separate clouds for the valance.)

2 Draw a large oval on the poster board. Use a 5" half circle to create curves around the entire edges of the oval. Cut out the pattern.

3 Use the pattern to cut two layers of quilt batt and white felt. Cut a slit in the center of one piece of white felt. This will be the back of the valance.

4 Layer the quilt batt on top of the felt pieces. Sew a ½" seam all the way around the cloud. Turn through the slit. Smooth with your fingers. Sew the slit shut.

5 With a needle and thread, sew stars to the valance. Make small thread loops at the back of the cloud, in the middle, and at the ends. Use small hooks to attach it to the wall just above the drapery rod.

6 For the clouds on the bottom of the curtain panels, repeat the same technique as for the valance. Sew the clouds to the bottom of the panels, while slightly gathered.

SIMPLE CURTAIN PANEL

YOU WILL NEED:

- 4½ yards cotton or polycotton fabric (add 6" to the required curtain panel length and double for each panel for larger windows)
- Drapery rod and hardware
- Mathcing threads

Tools: Scissors, sewing machine, iron and ironing board, measuring tape, pins.

1 Cut the fabric into three equal lengths of 54".

2 Cut one fabric piece in half lengthwise.

3 With right sides together, sew each half piece to a full length of fabric, creating two panels 67½" wide by 54" long.

4 Press a ½" narrow hem along all four sides. Press again a ½" hem along the longer sides. Topstitch.

5 Press a bottom hem of 1½" and a top hem of 2½". Topstitch. Press the panels.

6 Attach the rod brackets to the window.

7 Slide the panels on the rod, and attach them to the window.

More Thoughts

SINCE BABIES SPEND SO MUCH TIME LOOKING UP, PAINT THE CEILING BLUE AND ADD CLOUDS AND STARS. PAINT THE FURNITURE WITH THE SAME COLORS, AS SHOWN IN THE ROOM. ADD STARS SPRINKLED HERE AND THERE. CUT A SLIT IN THE FRONT OF A CLOUD. MAKE A COUPLE OF EXTRA ELEPHANTS AND GIRAFFES FROM THE SAIL AWAY WALL HANGING (PAGE 80). STICK THEM IN THE SLITS. THERE ARE NO LIMITS TO THE WHIMSICAL EFFECTS THAT CAN BE ADDED TO A NURSERY.

B Is for Baby

In this soft and sophisticated nursery, the walls are completely papered in a subtle stripe. A strip of wallpaper was cut to create a horizontal border. The border was stenciled with the alphabet, a classic motif for a child's room. Before buying the paper for this technique, ask for a small sample to test. I used a good heavy quality paper, and the acrylic paint adhered very nicely. Once it was dry for a couple of days, it was permanently set on the wallpaper.

The window panel was purchased and given a custom treatment by adding grosgrain ribbon to the tabs. The attractive rod was created inexpensively and easily with wood dowel and blocks. The wood alphabet letters centered over top add the final touch.

The design of this room, with its quiet elegance, offers a retreat for parents and baby. The alphabet design is a comforting presence that connects us all, whatever our age. Reciting the ABCs is an integral part of any childhood. Share the memories with your little one. A is for Apple, B is for …

Nursery Décor

WALL BORDER

SIZE: 6½" WIDE

YOU WILL NEED:

- 6½" wide wallpaper strips for border (three 15-foot lengths should be enough for an average size room)
- 5" stencil letter kit

- Burnt Umber acrylic paint
- ½" stencil brush

Tools: Scissors, tape, paper towel, pencil, ruler.

1 Review Stenciling on page 19 before you begin.

2 Measure to center the letters on the border strips. (The wallpaper chosen for this room had stripes 1" wide, so a stripe was used as the line to stencil on.)

3 Stencil the letters in order. Let the wallpaper strips dry for a couple of days. Wallpaper the rest of the room so it's also very dry before you apply the alphabet strip border.

4 When applying the border strips, instead of immersing them in water, wipe the back with a very damp cloth to activate the glue. Apply them to the wall.

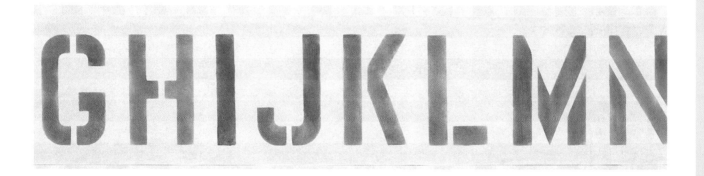

More Thoughts

STENCIL THE ALPHABET LETTERS ON DRESSER DRAWERS OR CLOSET DOORS. SPELL OUT YOUR BABY'S NAME, OR PLACE LETTERS IN A RANDOM ORDER. STENCIL ON PAPER AND FRAME SEVERAL LETTERS TO CREATE A SPECIAL WORD OR NAME. TWENTY-SIX LETTERS, UNLIMITED POSSIBILITIES.

The panels created for this nursery were purchased ready made and customized to coordinate with the room. Grosgrain ribbon used in projects for this room was also fused to the tabs of the panels. The rod is an easy inexpensive project that sets off the window panels very effectively. Panels were hung above the window because of the tabs. They look better against the wall than the window frame.

YOU WILL NEED:

- 1" dowel in length required for window
- 2 oz. black acrylic paint
- Clear acrylic varnish
- Two 2" to 3" wood blocks
- 5" "A," "B," and "C" wood letters
- 2 hooks

Tools: Foam brush, wood glue, sandpaper, pencil, ruler.

1 Lightly sand the letters and blocks.

2 Paint the blocks, dowel, hooks, and letters with two coats of black paint. Let dry thoroughly.

3 Finish all pieces with two coats of varnish.

4 Affix the hooks to the wall at either end of the window. These will hold the rod. Slide the panels on the rod. Place the rod above the window.

5 Glue the blocks to the wall at either end of the dowel rod, so they rest against the ends of the dowel. It should look like the blocks are holding the rod in place. (The rod can be lifted easily up off the hooks to slide the curtain off for laundering.)

6 Glue letters centered above the rod.

More Thoughts

THIS WINDOW TREATMENT COULD BE APPLIED TO A CLOSET OPENING. ADD PANELS AS NEEDED FOR A SLIGHT FULLNESS. USE MORE LETTERS OF THE ALPHABET OVER THE TOP OF THE PANELS. THERE IS ALWAYS ONE MORE IDEA FOR A PROJECT.

Notes

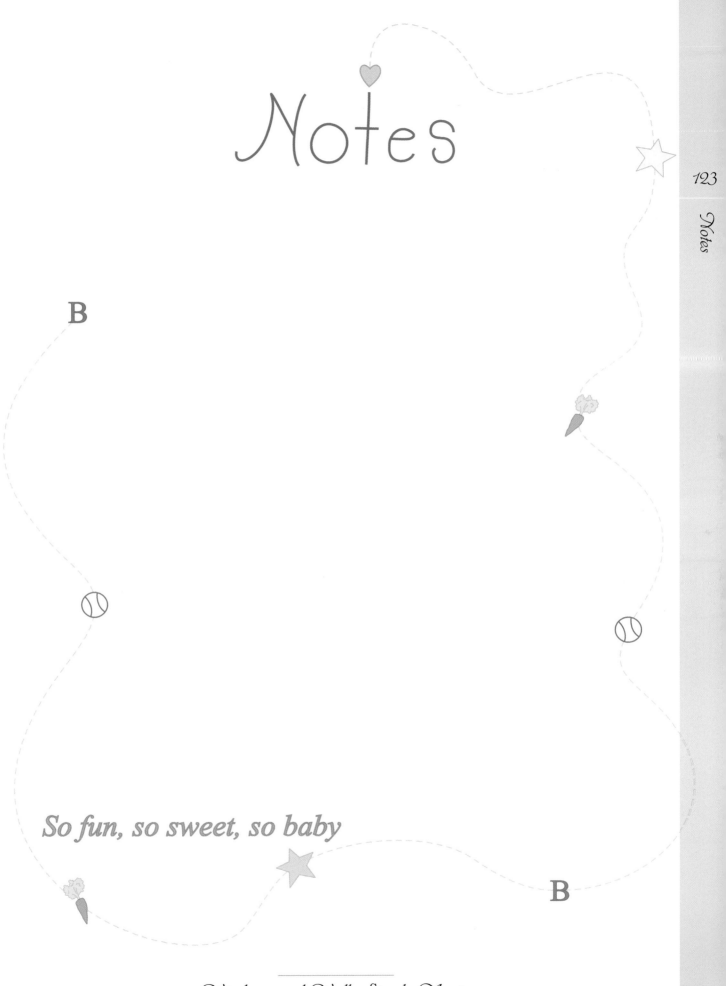

So fun, so sweet, so baby

Pattern Sheet Index and Project Numbers

Chapters are denoted by the symbols on the pattern sheet. Cut one pattern piece, reverse, and cut one more piece where indicated by (R) on the pattern sheet. Felt and fur colors are indicated by abbreviations on each piece.

Chapter 2: The Enchanted Garden
1 Bedtime Bunnies
2 Garden Lap Quilt
3 Ruffled Lamp*
4 Flowerpot Picture Frame
5 Cinderbella
6 Stuffed Carrot
7 Bunny with Chicks
8 Braided Bunny Rug
9 Flower Memo Holder
10 Baby Flops Bunny

Chapter 3: Boys, Bears, and Baseball
1 Benjamin Bear
2 Baseball Throw
3 Waggles the Puppy
4 Baseball Toy Holder
5 Sports Pillows
6 Tiny Teddy
7 "Let's Play Ball" Pillows
8 Diaper Stacker
9 Bat and Ball

Chapter 4: Sail Away on a Sea of Stars
1 Animal Ark
2 "My Little Star" Frame*
3 Gentle Giraffe
4 Mouse on a Star Book Holder
5 "Here Come the Animals" Peg Shelf
6 Elvis the Elephant
7 Sleepy Mouse
8 Starry Dreams Mobile
9 Sail Away Wall Hanging

Chapter 5 "B Is for Baby"
1 Memory Box
2 Alphabet Blanket*
3 ABC Blocks*
4 "SHH" Wall Hanging^
5 D Is for Dog
6 ABC Tissue Cover
7 ABC Rug
8 Scotty
* These projects don't require pieces from the pattern sheet.

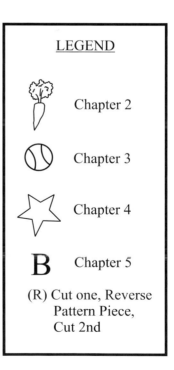

LEGEND

Chapter 2

Chapter 3

Chapter 4

B Chapter 5

(R) Cut one, Reverse
Pattern Piece,
Cut 2nd

Source Information

Support your local craft and fabric retailers. If you're unable to find a particular product, contact the manufacturer to locate a store or mail order source.

Adhesive Technologies (glue guns, glue sticks)
(800) 544-1021, www.adhesivetech.com

Beacon Chemical Company, Inc. (Fabri-Tac glue)
(800) 865-7238, www.beacon1.com

Behr (Kids' Color Collection paints)
(800) 854-0133 Ext.2, www.behrpaint.com

Coats & Clark (embroidery floss, upholstery thread)
(800) 648-1479, www.coatsandclark.com

Colonial Needle Company (sharps, soft sculpture, embroidery needles)
(914) 946-7474, www.colonialneedle.com

DecoArt Inc. (acrylic paints, varnish)
(800) 367-3047, www.decoart.com

Fiskars (Softgrip, Wave, Scallop Scissors, MicroTip Scissors, rotary cutters, self healing mats, rulers)
(715) 842-2091, www.fiskars.com

International Wallcoverings Company (Bears and Company-Second Edition borders and papers)
(905) 791-1547

John Bead Corp. Ltd. (safety eyes, eye beads, chenille stems, variety of craft supplies)
(888) 545-9999, www.johnbead.com

Kunin Felt (Rainbow Classic Felt, Plush Felt, Shaggy Plush Felt)
(800) 292-7900, www.kuninfelt.com

Plaid Enterprises, Inc. (stencils)
(770) 923-8200, www.plaid.com

STYROFOAM* (foam balls, eggs, discs, blocks, cones, stars, hearts)
www.dow.com/craft
*Trademark of The Dow Chemical Company

Therm O Web (HeatnBond Ultrahold Iron-On Adhesive, Lite Iron-On, PeelnStick Double-Sided Adhesive)
(847) 520-5200, www.thermoweb.com

Walnut Hollow (wood products)
(800) 950-5101, www.walnuthollow.com

Warm Company (polyester fiberfill, batting and pillow forms)
(800) 234-9276, www.warmcompany.com

About the Author

Debra Quartermain is an enthusiastic and energetic designer who delights in sharing her creativity. Her whimsical designs are found in magazines, books, project sheets, and her own pattern line. Her favorite techniques include sewing, soft sculpture, embroidery, stenciling, scrapbooking, floral arranging, and interior decorating.

Debra has taught classes in sewing and crafting at several fabric and craft shops for over 10 years. At the present time, her main teaching focus is with children in a craft club at her daughter's elementary school. She believes the joy of creating needs to be nurtured and encouraged in children by providing them with skills, products, and endless possibilities.

From childhood, Debra has had a sewing machine close by. While her mother sewed, Debra practiced her earliest techniques with doll clothes. Through her sewing, she has created entire wardrobes for herself and her children, and decorated her home with things from pillows and curtains to life-sized dolls, animals, and snowmen. Her combination of sewing and decorating skills are found in many homes and businesses.

During the last four years, a menagerie of soft fuzzy animals, particularly bears, has taken over her life, as her pattern and kit line is sold from Australia, the United States, and Canada to Great Britain. Their sweet expressions touch the heart and bring a smile. Through all of her designs, Debra's main wish is for everyone to be inspired to explore their talents and realize their own unique creativity. She wrote this book as a wonderful opportunity for imagination to become a reality where anyone can easily create the baby nursery of their dreams.

Debra lives in the small village of New Maryland in NB, Canada, with her two wonderful daughters, Amanda and Katy, and a menagerie of friends, stuffed and otherwise, from a "teddy" hamster to cats, a dog, and an orphan red squirrel.